Management in the Hotel and Catering Industry

Harold V Gullen and
Geoffrey E Rhodes

Batsford Academic and Educational Ltd   London

First published 1983
Reprinted 1990

Typeset by Tek-Art Ltd, Kent
and printed in Great Britain by
Billing & Son Ltd
Worcester
for the publishers
B T Batsford Limited
4 Fitzhardinge Street
London W1H 0AH

British Library Cataloguing in Publication Data

Gullen, Harold V.
    Management in the hotel and catering industry.
    1. Hotels, taverns, etc. – Management – Great Britain
    2. Catering and catering industries – Management,
    Great Britain
    I. Title   II. Rhodes, Geoffrey E.
    647'.94'068   TX911.3.M27

ISBN 0 7134 1932 6

Introduction

This book is intended for those coming to a study of the principles and
techniques of management for the first time, whether as students at
Ordinary or Higher TEC levels, on NEBSS courses, as undergraduates in
Hotel and Catering subjects or as post-graduate students undertaking a
concentrated course to prepare them for entry into the industry following
their first degree studies.

Its purpose is to provide an overview of management rather than a
detailed presentation of all aspects of managerial activity, which is
beyond the scope of this work, but references have been provided in the
text to which those interested in particular topics can refer.

It is also anticipated that certain topic areas may be of interest to
practising managers in the Hotel and Catering Industry.

Contents

1
Management

1 MANAGEMENT AS A CONCEPT

What is a manager?

Faced with this question, many would respond that a manager is someone responsible for getting things done. Further questions would probably result in the views that managers are those who:

(a) control other people and

(b) operate in an organisation of some sort.

We are familiar with the word 'manager' and know of shop managers, departmental managers, restaurant managers, hotel managers and so on. In many situations, faced with a problem or difficulty, it is the manager we want to see. The manager is therefore someone we see as having power and authority to make things happen, and in most instances they make things happen through their subordinates, usually by telling them what is to be done to deal with a particular situation, problem or difficulty.

It is important to grasp this principle, namely that managers cause things to happen through the agency of other people in an organisation.

The feature common to managers, supervisors, foremen, charge hands, etc, is that they have subordinates to whom they can issue instructions and whose activities they have the power to control. For purposes of clarity we shall use the term 'manager' to indicate a person who is in a position of authority over a subordinate. Thus the word 'manager' can be used to describe someone at quite low levels in the organisation and embraces all the titles (and others) listed at the beginning of this paragraph.

2 MANAGEMENT AS AN ACTIVITY

What is management, and what do managers do?

Management texts often give either a formal definition of management, for example BRECH[1], or in many other cases a description of the management activity and the functions undertaken by those we call managers.

In either case, what is noticeable is that many of the words and phrases used are common to the various authors. Some of the terms commonly used are mentioned below with brief comments against each of them:

management process –a movement forward over a period of time involving
people and departmental groups who must work

	together eg. Reception, Restaurants, Kitchens, Accommodation Services, etc
objectives –	the situations companies are trying to achieve through the activities of managers
planning –	the laying down of courses of action designed to achieve objectives or results, eg sales performance, occupancy levels, economical uses of resources, etc
control –	of peoples' performance in relation to the plans mentioned above and the comparison of what is actually achieved with the planned objectives or targets
organisation –	the assignment of duties to people as individuals and their formation into groups to achieve specific tasks or objectives creates the organisational framework of the unit
co-ordination –	the synchronisation of work which has been subdivided between subordinates to ensure that the varied sections of the whole organisation combine effectively to achieve their combined purpose
communication –	the means by which co-ordination is achieved
motivation –	persuading subordinates to work enthusiastically and conscientiously to achieve the tasks allocated to them.

3 SCHOOLS OF MANAGEMENT

There are many definitions of management ranging from the formal one mentioned above to short statements such as 'Management is getting things done through people' or 'Management is decision making'.

Approaches to the analysis of management as an activity are many and a number of different schools of thought concerning the management process have developed over the last hundred years. A brief outline of some of them is given below and those interested should refer to HICKS[2].

3.1 The Traditional school

This approach stresses that management is best seen as a process of getting things done through people organised in formal groups and that activities such as planning, organising, motivating controlling and communicating can be defined and studied. This school is concerned with the identification of principles concerning organisations and management which can be studied as a means of improving the practice of management. It also sees management as a universal process having some applicability to any type of organisation.

3.2 The Empirical school

Here the concern has been to study managerial experience as a means of deducing principles from analysis of the successes and failures of the past, on the grounds that such precedents will be a useful guide to action when considered in conjunction with a manager's own experience. There is, unfortunately, no guarantee that the circumstances of the past will ever be precisely replicated in the present or future, and it could be foolhardy to place too much reliance on past experience.

3.3 The Human Relations school

The emphasis here is on the relationship between members of an organisation, where the manager is seen as a leader and motivator of the individuals and groups he controls. There is concern that people should be seen as individuals and that consideration be given to their needs, hopes and aspirations.

3.4 The Decision-Theory school

This approach concentrates on the multitude of decisions made by managers in an organisation and is concerned with the decision making process being a rational activity whereby the best solution is selected from a range of possible solutions.

3.5 The Formalism school

This school of thought proposes that people in an organisation respond and perform best when it is clearly indicated to them where they stand in the hierarchy of the organisation, ie who their superior is, who their subordinates are, and where it is clearly demonstrated to them exactly what it is they are required to do, ie they are provided with a Job Description.

4 THE MANAGEMENT ENVIRONMENT

In looking at managers and management up to this point, the context has been that of the organisation in which management takes place. Certainly managers do operate within an internal environment, but the greater, external environment must also be taken into account for a proper understanding of all the factors which influence managerial situations.

The two aspects will be considered separately:

4.1 The internal environment

Within the organisation there are many factors which influence a manager and a number of constraints within which he must operate. Internally, a manager is concerned with resources and their use to achieve the objectives of the organisation and to a significant extent these are controllable by management. These resources are:

(a) *human*: having the knowledge, skills and experience to bring to the working situation: the ability to cook, sell, serve, operate a bar efficiently and so on. Management needs people as individuals and in groups to work with and to use effectively the resources of the organisation.

(b) *non-human*: the building, the hotel, café, restaurant or motel and the land on which it stands; the plant and equipment ranging from cookers and ovens to bed linen and napery, cutlery, furniture, etc. Other resources include finance to provide working capital to meet expenses, to pay wages and to ensure an adequate supply of new materials.

Resources, both physical and human must be managed in the light of the organisation's policies and procedures, in order to maximise performance for the achievement of the objectives (financial or otherwise) of the organisation.

4.2 The external environment

All organisations operate in and are affected by the external environment which can sometimes be favourable to the achievement of the objectives of the organisation and at other times make that achievement more difficult; in either case, it is outside the control of management. The manager must therefore take account of the external environment in carrying out the elements of a manager's task as described above. He must identify the factors in the environment which impinge on future strategies and planning and on present operations, so that he can consider what opportunities or constraints these factors present.

4.2.1 *The economy*

The hotel and catering industry has many sectors which can be affected to differing degrees by the state of the economy. Welfare and institutional catering are, at the time of writing, being massively affected by the moves to reduce public sector spending. Some local authorities have changed the type of school meals offered in order to achieve a less labour-intensive service. Regional hospital boards have examined hospital catering to reduce costs by evaluating whether 'buy-in' policies are preferable to running departments such as bakeries and butcheries, whether vending machines can be brought in to take the place of shift-working catering staff, and introducing cafeteria service in place of waiter service. Sectors of the industry which cater for 'eating-out' are perhaps among the first to be affected by the reduction of spare cash in the pockets of people experiencing leaner times during a recession. In an expanding, buoyant economy it is likely that there would be freer spending and that sales would be expected to rise. It is also likely that the greater amount of profit opportunity will result in keener competition.

The response of the manager who is aware of the effects of the economy on his organisation will be mainly in his approach to budgeting for the coming year. If the economy is affected by inflation, then he must decide, on the information he has collected, how much increase in future costs to budget for. If the organisation has significant overseas tourist trade, then the foreign exchange rate will have an effect on future plans. If this effect is interpreted as a probable reduction in overseas guests, then what must be done to fill that gap with other business? Similarly, the indications of a change in the economy for the better would be noted and planning decisions made which would enable the organisation to share in the economic upturn.

This topic of environmental awareness and the making of decisions based upon such study will be returned to in chapter 10 when aspects of decision making are discussed.

4.2.2 *Labour supply*

Any organisation needs access to a pool of labour with varying degrees of skill. Some work in kitchens can be carried out by workers with little or no expertise, or with a minimum of training. Other jobs in the industry require a high level of training, skill and experience. In times of high unemployment as at present, this concern of management may assume less importance with large numbers of skilled and unskilled labour available on the market, but plans for changes and expansion would need to take into account the availability or non-availability of people with the required skills.

Absence of such skills need not mean that development cannot take place, as training or retraining of existing staff can be undertaken, or in a large organisation it may be possible to transfer staff from other units to provide the expertise.

4.2.3 *Legal/political environment*

The manager in the hotel and catering industry, as in many other industries must operate within a complex system of legal requirements and constraints covering many aspects of his operation. In so far as employees are concerned, the provisions of the Trades Union and Labour Relations Act, the Equal Opportunities Act and the Employment Protection Act, for example, must be borne in mind. Employees and guests are protected by Fire Regulations; the provision of intoxicating drinks is controlled through licences issued by local magistrates; a major item of expense is the rate levied by the local authority; profits are affected by legislation in respect of taxation, and sales may be influenced by the rate at which Value Added Tax is levied. Recent increases in the 'fast food' and 'take-away' style of operation have largely resulted from the increase in the rate of VAT from 8% to 15% in 1979. This caused an increase in the total cost of meals to consumers, with a consequent fall off in demand. This the industry has sought to offset by varying the meals and services and their style of presentation.

Here, too, can be considered the influence of Trades Unions on the manager. As yet the unions are not very strongly represented in the Private Sector of the industry. On the other hand, in the Public Sector, for example in hospitals there is a much higher incidence of union membership amongst employees and this can have a significant affect on managers and on the style and approach they adopt in dealing with and controlling subordinates.

4.2.4 *Competition*

The Private Sector of the industry operates in a highly competitive environment; even in times of extremely high demand for its services or where there is little alternative provision, a constant watch over the competitive situation is essential. The quality of competitors' products and services, the range of products and services supplied, the particular classes of clientele they are seeking to attract and the prices they are charging should be the subject of constant monitoring. Attempting to maintain a position in the market, attempting merely to maintain the *status quo* usually results in a deterioration of the market position as competitors progress and improve their position. This aspect will be dealt with more fully in the next chapter in relation to objective setting in relation to market standing (section 2.1).

4.2.5 *Suppliers*

Reliable service and appropriate quality standards from suppliers would clearly benefit the management of any enterprise. But such desirable features of the relationships between purchasing organisations and suppliers do not arise by luck, but must be planned for and fostered.

Disparity in the relative sizes of purchasing firms and supplying firms may affect the development of such relationships – a large supplier, for example, may be thought to be indifferent to the behaviour or reaction of a small buying organisation and a small supplier be overawed by an order from a large customer. What must be remembered, however, is that organisations do not form relationships. It is people within organisations whose activities and methods of working become known to the people they deal with in other organisations who are mainly responsible, for good or ill, for the development of inter-company relations.

The purchasing organisation which issues clear orders, allows a reasonable time for delivery and abides by the credit period agreed with the supplier, is likely to be best served by suppliers. Before a purchasing organisation could achieve these ideals, the management would have to arrive at a well-designed purchasing procedure, be in control of activities by sound pre-planning and be in a well-managed cash position. If these are the normal conditions, then temporary falls from grace such as the urgent order because of an oversight, or the extension of credit facilities for a period longer than that agreed, will be catered for by the well-disposed supplier.

Another aspect of the relationship with suppliers is that of the rights of the buyer – to expect delivery promises to be kept and to receive goods of the agreed quality and specifications. A buyer in good standing and enjoying good relations with the supplier should expect good levels of service – but it would be foolish to assume this and not to set up control procedures to progress deliveries and check goods received.

Further discussion on the selection of suppliers and related purchasing procedures will be given in chapter 8.

4.2.6 *Shareholders*
It is not within the scope of this book to discuss the various types of shares and shareholders. In the context of a review of factors in the management environment, it is felt sufficient to mention the responsibility borne by management for the husbandry of shareholders' money. This responsibility led ROBERT HELLER to formulate as his first of 'Ten Truths of Management', 'Think before you Act: the Money isn't Yours'.[3].

Yet, even when a conscientious manager is fully aware of the necessity to provide the shareholder with a reasonable return on investment, the fact is that most managerial decisions have outcomes at some future time and the future is always uncertain. The manager demonstrates his conscientiousness by his efforts in collecting information relevant to the decision area and by his readiness to use techniques which increase the chances of favourable outcomes to the decisions he makes.

4.2.7 *Technology*
In common with every other industry, the hotel and catering industry has available developments in technology which must be examined by the industry's managements to see what benefits may be derived and what changes in both operational activities and associated control procedures may be involved.

There are three, broad areas of technological development which could be considered in the context of this review of external factors affecting management:
1 developments in the availability and improved quality of pre-prepared, convenience foods
2 developments in kitchen equipment and food preparation systems
3 developments in the speedy processing of information.

The first and second of these areas have implications regarding the skill levels and numbers of food preparation staff required compared to traditionally operated kitchens.

The third area has important effects upon management. Micro-computers bring data processing capability of a very useful order indeed, within the purchasing power of many a householder, let alone companies, to provide sound bases for managerial decision making with a facility and at a cost which would have been unbelievable even five years ago.

5 SUMMARY
This chapter has concerned itself with a brief look at management as a concept and as an activity; some of the schools of management thought have been mentioned and the environments and constraints within which a manager must operate have been outlined.

Throughout this introductory chapter, a number of terms forming part of the 'language' or 'jargon' of management have been used, but with no

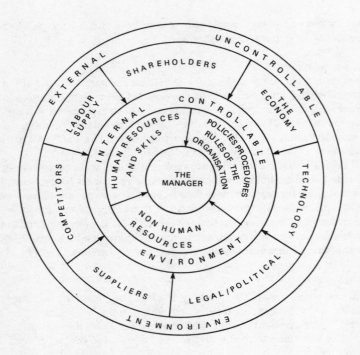

Figure 1   The manager's environment

attempt to explain them in detail at this stage. Most of these terms – planning, organising, decision making and so on – are words familiar to us. In the context of the management activity, they assume more specialised and specific meanings, and in the following chapters these, and other terms and activities will be considered and expanded in appropriate depth.

References
[1] BRECH, E F L, *Management its Nature and Significance* p17, Pitman Paperbacks, 1968
[2] HICKS, H G, *The Management of Organisations; A Systems and Human Resources Approach,* pp 377-383, McGraw Hill Book Co, New York, 1972
[3] HELLER, R, *The Naked Manager,* p 245, Barrie and Jenkins, London, 1972.

2
Objectives and objective setting

1 THE NATURE OF ORGANISATIONAL OBJECTIVES

Without an objective, or objectives, there is no reason why an organisation should exist or be brought into being. Organisations comprise people working together to achieve some purpose or goal which they would not be able to achieve separately. It should be noted that the terms goal, target, purpose and mission are frequently used interchangeably with objective in management literature.

The formulation of objectives for a commercial organisation is usually the responsibility of the board of directors, or its equivalent and it is they who, in the light of the total environment, internal and external, in which the organisation is situated at a particular time, decide what the objectives of the organisation are to be.

MASSIE and DOUGLAS[1] say that '... objectives are ideas and statements which give the direction and goal to behaviour and effort'. If, for example, the board of a company operating a chain of restaurants decides that over the next five years it will open two new restaurants a year, then that will be one of the company's objectives. It then becomes necessary for the management of that company to be told of the objective and for them to understand what behaviour and effort is required of them, and their subordinates for the achievement of that objective. Managers will, in fact, have to start to make plans to achieve the objective. The planning aspect of management will be dealt with more fully in chapter 4, but is mentioned now so that the relationship between objective setting and planning is clear from the outset.

Objectives are future-oriented in that they represent what it is intended and hoped will be achieved, usually within a specified period of time. Although expressed as aspirations and hopes, objectives should be capable of realisation and attainment. This requires of management a realistic appraisal of the external environment, the competition, the economy, the cost of borrowing money or the time to obtain any planning permission which may be necessary, and all the other factors impinging on the choice of objectives. A clear assessment of the strengths and weaknesses of the company itself, in relation to staff and all other resources is also essential. Environments, however, are not static but change and develop over time; it, follows therefore that a company's objectives must be subject to modification in a changing world.

The most common answer to the question 'what should an

organisation's objective be?' is usually 'Profit'. In a commercial, competitive environment, it is true that in the long run sufficient profits must be earned to enable the company to survive; employees require to be paid as do suppliers; shareholders expect to receive a dividend on the money they have invested, and repairs, renewals and investment in new equipment have to be paid for. For these purposes, adequate profits are essential. In the non-competitive sectors of the industry, the objectives may not be profit. Hospital catering, school meals and industrial canteens will not be expected to generate profit. Nevertheless, objectives will be set for management to achieve, for example to feed patients at a cost of not more than x per day, or to cover the cost of raw materials in the revenue obtained, say, in a works canteen. Whatever the objectives, they should be expressed in measurable terms so that progress towards them can be measured.

The time-scale of objectives may be long or short. The objective of the company mentioned above which wants to open more restaurants is long term; the same company could have as another objective increasing the number of customers from an average of x customers to y customers every day. Each of these is equally valid as an objective and equally capable of being measured, which is an important aspect of managerial control.

In addition to the type of objective mentioned above, organisations have responsibilities to the community at large. All organisations have the objective of survival and, through survival, to continue to provide employment to those who work for them – an important purpose in itself. What survival also ensures, is that by continuing to operate, the organisation buys goods from other companies, pays rates to the local authority and taxes to the government. In so doing it helps to maintain the fabric of our society. Organisations have responsibility too, not to cause pollution to the environment in which we all must live; they therefore have certain social responsibilities which must be borne in mind when objectives are being formulated, and plans for their realisation laid down.

In terms of general objectives it can be said that they:
(a) are normally determined by the board
(b) are the basis for planning
(c) should ensure the long-term survival of the business
(d) may not always be profit oriented
(e) should be measurable and attainable
(f) entail considerations of social responsibility.

There is not just one level of objective setting in an organisation. The main, broad objectives set to give direction to the organisation as a whole will be sub-divided into departmental objectives, further broken down into sectional objectives and finally assigned to staff on an individual basis. At each of these levels those involved should be aware of how their work contributes to the sectional, departmental and organisational objectives.

2 AREAS OF OBJECTIVE SETTING IN THE HOTEL AND CATERING INDUSTRY

There are a number of areas in which any business should determine its objectives. DRUCKER[2] lists these areas in his *Practice of Management* and it is this framework which will be adopted in looking at objective setting in the hotel and catering industry.

2.1 Market standing

All organisations have a market or clientele for the product or service they are offering; a market consists of people and might comprise school children, workers in a factory, patients in a hospital, lunchers or diners in a restaurant or residents in an hotel. It is the type of customer which broadly determines the nature and quality of the product or service which is offered, and one cannot be considered in isolation from the other, since each affects the other. The type of guest using a luxury hotel in Park Lane has different requirements from those of a person seeking one star accommodation, and the quality and price of products and service will reflect this difference.

Decisions have to be taken by companies in the private hotel and restaurant sector as to the type of market (people) they see as their principal source of business. To do this effectively, they will need information as to the number of such potential clients in order to determine the nature of the products and services required to satisfy their needs.

The situations of existing organisations are, of course, different from those which have not yet commenced operating, and in the former case, a great deal of information will already be available in the form of existing records. In the latter case a complete Feasibility Study might be required involving research into the area in which it is proposed to locate the unit, the potential sources of demand within that area, the facilities which are currently being provided by those who would be competitors, the number of potential users for the type and quality of product the company has in mind. It is not possible to develop a discussion of Feasibility Studies here, but those interested should refer to DOSWELL[3] or KOTAS[4] for fuller treatments.

In examining either situation, it should be remembered that to survive and be profitable, customers must be offered that which they want. Only when customers' wants and needs have been clearly identified can the appropriate product/service be offered to them. It is not a case of deciding that a particular product/service can be conveniently provided using existing resources, and then hoping to persuade people to buy it. It is a case of identifying peoples' needs and then filling them.

Businesses operate in a competitive environment and decisions concerning customer/product relationships cannot be made without taking this into account. There is no advantage in producing and supplying goods and services which are identical to those being provided by established competitors (unless unsatisfied demand is identified). In these circumstances trade can only be gained by enticing customers away from the competitors, and usually this can be achieved only by offering the consumer a price advantage. This might lead to intensive price competition from which no one benefits.

A more sensible approach is to look for a market which is not currently being supplied, establish that the market is sufficiently large and then to promote the 'different' nature of your offering.

In terms of the marketing aspect, it is desirable to set objectives taking into account the factors described above in order to provide the necessary direction to the company. For example:

to identify the requirements of customers/guests.

to satisfy those requirements.

to promote (advertise) the products/services to customers/guests

are examples of such objectives, and, when laid down by the board do give clear guidance to management in the conduct of the business. Once established, objectives in relation to marketing govern the total activities of the business, which must be geared to the attainment of the objectives. It is stressed again, that we live and work in a changing world and that in consequence, objectives should not be seen as fixed and immutable, but as being subject to change and amendment as the market situation requires. This necessitates information being available to management on an on-going basis.

2.2 Innovation

Innovation – the alteration of, or changes to, that which is already established, or the introduction of something new – is inescapable given the need for flexibility in a dynamic situation, and there are two aspects to innovation which can be considered separately.

2.2.1 Products and services

Products and services have a life expectancy of very variable length; like people, they are born, come to maturity and ultimately die. The era of the great railway hotels started to decline with the development of the motorway network and its associated motel type of operation. Prior to, and immediately after the second world war the principal means of crossing the Atlantic was the large ocean liner – the Queen Elizabeth, United States and France to give but three examples. The advent and development of large jet aircraft quickly rendered the ocean liner obsolete, largely because of its slowness.

So it is with the hotel trade; styles and fashions in decor and service change. The traditional 'product' of Bed and Breakfast has been replaced by 'Bed' with Breakfast as an optional extra, or in continental form. Fast food provision has assumed increasing importance in recent years. Management therefore needs to be always watchful and to have the objective of being ready to replace or revise and adapt their products as and when the situation requires. This is something which needs to be planned for in advance, and replacements, or at least ideas for replacement products, should be constantly part of the management's thinking, so that as one product loses its appeal, decor needs renewing or menus need changing, there is something ready.

The implementation of such changes is, it should be mentioned, an excellent opportunity to obtain publicity for the unit, but this too requires advance planning.

2.2.2 *Staff*
The nature of objective setting as it affects managers and workers is discussed in sections 2.6 and 2.7 of this chapter. The achievement of objectives may well require a change in the activities, location or attitude of those involved, and innovation implies change. Managers need to be able to recognise both the need to change and adjust themselves, and also to be able to motivate staff and to overcome their resistance to proposed changes.

In rapidly changing technological, legal, political, economic and competitive environments, managers must accept that both they and their subordinates may need re-training on a periodic basis to enable them to work with economy and efficiency. In short they must accept new methods, ideas and approaches as circumstances require.

2.3 **Productivity**
The setting of objectives under the heading of productivity involves an audit of the resources used to achieve organisational aims and plans aimed at increasing the value of the goods and services produced from those resources.

A distinction between higher production and higher productivity must be appreciated. If a hundred meals are produced for a labour cost of £10 and two hundred meals for a labour cost of £20 then the production has doubled but productivity has remained the same in terms of labour input. If, through application of improved methods of food production, the two hundred meals were produced for a labour cost of, say, £16 then that would indicate an increase in the productivity of labour.

The audit of resources mentioned above is an exercise which should lead to constructive thinking about ways of increasing the productivity of all the significant groups of resources used by an organisation. The first stage is to identify the resources used, and a listing of these would include items such as land, buildings, equipment, stocks (food, liquor, linen, etc) cash and labour. The listing represents an analysis of resources, so that the massive and rather formless task of seeking productivity improvements can be better ordered and focussed upon one resource at a time for the purpose of stimulating ideas on possible ways to increase the productivity of each resource.

The following examples are given to illustrate this approach:

(a) *Buildings* Are we recovering the costs of rent, rates, lighting and heating the space within our present building as well as we might? Are there areas not earning revenue which, with a given investment, could be converted into revenue earning rooms?

(b) *Equipment* Is our equipment suited to the uses to which it is being put? Are our methods of working more labour-intensive than they need be because of the type of equipment in use? Are we incurring excessive costs because equipment is not being regularly maintained?

(c) *Cash* What investment opportunities are available to us which will provide an adequate return on our cash resources?

(d) *Stocks* Are the total costs of ordering and stock-holding at a minimum? For those stocks representing the bulk of our investment in stock, have the principles of stock control been used to arrive at optimum levels?

It can be seen that these illustrations are in the form of questions and that it would be a rare organisation where the answers to these questions could be given immediately and with justified confidence in the accuracy of the answers. Yet a management which adopts this analysis of resources and, after asking questions along the lines indicated, seeks to find the answers to the questions, is surely on the way to discovering ways of improving the use of the resources for which they bear responsibility.

The question of labour productivity has been purposely ignored in this section for two reasons:

(i) the complex factors involved in labour productivity will be dealt with separately in chapter 9 on Work Study, and

(ii) it was thought desirable to establish that the problem of achieving higher levels of productivity is not simply a matter of urging the labour force to greater efforts. In recent years there has been a tendency for politicians and the leaders of management associations to deplore the low level of productivity in British industry and to imply that large sections of the working population are responsible because of their lack of the will to work. This view ignores the management responsibility for securing the best return possible on all the other important resources apart from labour. It also ignores the fact that an organisation which is competently managed in all respects is unlikely to have any problems with regard to the productivity of its work force.

2.4 Physical and financial resources

The interdependence of these areas for objectives setting is most clearly appreciated under the heading of physical and financial resources. Plans made and objectives set under 'market standing' and 'innovation' could not be realistically arrived at without full consideration of the constraints imposed by current physical and financial resources.

Examples of such constraints are:

— size and layout of the present premises

- the number of staff currently employed
- the skills and experience of present staff
- the amount of capital available to support stated marketing objectives
- the amount of capital available to afford re-equipping programmes necessary to achieving new systems of operating and new procedures.

It is not, however, simply a matter of ensuring that present physical and financial resources are adequate to support objectives, and scrapping those objectives if inadequacy is detected. If that were the case, very little growth and development would take place. The task is to establish the costs of bringing the physical and financial resources up to the level required to support other objectives and, at the same time, maintain the financial stability of the organisation.

In its simplest terms, the maintenance of financial stability is achieved by being able to meet current liabilities from current assets – which normally means that an adequate supply of cash is available to satisfy creditors. Suppose that a marketing objective had been set which, in order for it to be achieved, would require an extension to the restaurant and additional costs from the employment of more staff. Before such an objective is agreed, we should sincerely hope that the market need for more restaurant business had been established and that sensible forecasts of increases in expected revenue had been computed. This necessary ground work then enables an investment appraisal to be carried out to establish the costs of the extension, the higher operating charges and the expected increases in revenue which will be the outcome of increasing the physical resource.

There are techniques of investment appraisal in management accounting which help in arriving at a decision in these cases, and also decision making techniques which would clarify the issues involved in formulating the marketing objective. These will be treated separately later in this book. There may exist entrepreneurs with great business flair who are able to commit organisations to massive expenditure and recoup substantial profits without using any formalised techniques to assist decision making, but it is as well to remember that the history of industry is frequently punctuated by spectacular collapses of the empires of entrepreneurs who were not quite so fortunate. In the very recent past one such organisation has failed with debts totalling £270 million pounds.

2.5 Profitability

Before considering the setting of objectives for profit it is necessary to recall the outcomes of the statements of objectives related to Marketing. As already stated, marketing objectives govern the activities to be undertaken by the organisation in terms such as the number of meals to be provided and the sales of accommodation planned. These levels of activity in turn dictate the requirements for the necessary inputs of space, finance, raw materials, labour and so on – in other words the total costs of achieving the desired outputs. Profit is thus going to be dependent upon how well those costs are controlled, how close actual sales are to those planned and what prices are being charged for the goods and services being sold. In the context of planning for a specified profit, then, management must have as guides:

(i)   an analysis of all costs which will be incurred, analysed departmentally
(ii) administrative and general costs fairly and consistently allocated to revenue earning departments
(iii) sales objectives analysed by product (food, beverages, accommodation, etc)
(iv) a calculation of expected profits derived from guides (i), (ii) and (iii).

At this stage in the profit planning exercise it could be revealed that the indicated level of profitability from certain activities is thought not to be satisfactory. Attention must then be given to the factors which lead to the derivation of the expected profit – the costs, the amount of sales and the selling price – all of which may be within the power of management to control more closely or change in order to improve profitability. If, after careful consideration, management conclude that these factors cannot be changed, then a partial re-writing of marketing objectives may be called for.

To be able to decide whether a given, expected profit is satisfactory or otherwise implies that some measure or standard of profitability exists which can be used as a yardstick. There are many ways of attempting to measure profitability and as many arguments both for and against each of those ways. For the purpose of arriving at a profitability objective, the total projected net profit for the enterprise may be expressed as a percentage of the capital employed (total assets less current liabilities). This gives a figure which could not be used to compare between-company results, unless a purposive, standard form of accounting had been adopted by the companies concerned, but will provide a control figure which enables management to detect any trend from one period to another if the control figure is calculated continuously. It is therefore an indicator of the progress of the company in terms of profit related to the capital invested and any downturn in the percentage figure is a signal for remedial action to be undertaken by management. If, by estimating the figure by means of projected profits, management receives a warning of a down turn before it actually happens, then it will serve a very useful purpose if effective re-thinking can avoid or, at least, mitigate, a fall in profitability.

The return on capital employed measure refers to the overall result of an organisation's trading. It must be supported by departmentalised measures of profitability if closer, effective control is to be achieved within the organisation. Departmental control ratios assist management to locate the areas where investigation is most urgently required when, for example, the return on capital ratio has indicated the need for remedial action. They also are the prime guides for departmental management as to the degree of success which they are achieving in managing their departments.

Commonly used departmental ratios are:

food cost to sales   stock values to sales
labour cost to sales   net profit to sales.

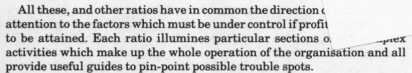

All these, and other ratios have in common the direction of attention to the factors which must be under control if profit is to be attained. Each ratio illumines particular sections of complex activities which make up the whole operation of the organisation and all provide useful guides to pin-point possible trouble spots.

It is so far assumed that the profit objective is highly desirable and that there could be no objection to the desire for profit. It is necessary to consider, however, the view point that if profit is the sole objective, then there could be danger. Possibly the only organisation which could survive if profit were the sole objective is the fly-by-night market trader who could move the scene of his operations about the country before dissatisfied customers could get at him. Profit as a sole objective must imply that considerations of value for money, customer service and customer satisfaction are ignored. Yet, as in most variables, a continuum exists with, at one extreme customer orientation and at the other, profit orientation. It is the policy of the management of a company which determines the positioning of that company along the continuum. The reader could no doubt mentally review organisations with which he has had contact as employee or as a customer and rank them as to their placings between customer and profit orientation extremes. Certainly in recent years there have been highly critical articles published about the over-charging of tourists by London hotels and restaurants and dire forecasts of the adverse effects of this on future tourist trade figures.

Finally, there are large, important sectors of the hotel and catering industry where no profit is possible because either no direct charge is made to the customer (hospital catering, for example) or the catering operation is subsidised, as in the case of industrial catering. It is clear that the management of such units must be responsible for operating within objectives set with respect to costs. There are normally in the form of budgets for raw materials, labour, fuel, administration and so on. It is therefore suggested that the managerial task of achieving the objectives of consumer service and satisfaction within specified cost constraints is in all respects except price, analogous to managing an operation to achieve a profit objective.

2.6 Manager performance and development

2.6.1 *Manager performance*

The measurement of the performance of a manager is more difficult than that of an employee who performs a given task with a concrete end product. The manager's performance is complicated by results being achieved through the work of the people over whom he has authority and by some results being abstract such as the achievement of good co-

.1ation in his area of responsibility or the maintenance of good staff elationships.

Yet it is self-evident that because managers are in key positions affecting the achievement of organisational objectives, any objectives-setting exercise must take into account the setting of objectives for the managers themselves. If these objectives are to be useful, then there must be developed some method of measuring a manager's performance against them, and that measurement must take into account the difficulties mentioned above. The system of Management by Objectives (MBO) is one method which many organisations have found helpful in both establishing the personal objectives of individual managers and also in taking into account the abstract results which, although they cannot be weighed or counted, can be vital to the task of the manager. While it is not being claimed that MBO is the only way for an organisation to be able to set managerial objectives and subsequently measure performance against them, the section on MBO (chapter 3) explores more fully the requirements and problems in this most important area of objectives setting.

2.6.2 *Manager development*
Assuming that an organisation has only those management levels and positions necessary to its effective operation, it is clearly important for the future of the organisation to ensure that plans for the development of managerial employees are established and acted upon.

Development needs can be established by evaluating the performance of individual managers against their objectives. The results of such an evaluation should reveal both the strengths and weaknesses of the managers concerned, so that strengths can be built upon, perhaps ear-marking the manager for future advancement, and weaknesses repaired by appropriate training or by supervised exposure to those areas in which the weaknesses or lack of experience have been identified.

Objectives setting in manager development is thus concerned with:
(i)   strengthening the capability of the management team, and
(ii) planning for a supply of managers of the appropriate level for the future.

2.7 **Worker performance and attitude**
2.7.1 *Worker performance*
Stated at its simplest, the setting of objectives for worker performance is determining the required number of people to carry out the work generated by the sales or service objectives of the organisation. Discovering what is the 'required' number of people quickly takes us away from simple concepts and demands answers to such questions as:
—   what methods and procedures will be followed in carrying out this work?
—   are the skills and knowledge of the workforce equal to the demands of the work?

- are our employees willing to follow the methods and procedures laid down?
- do we know what level of effort and application to work can be reasonably expected of our workforce?
- are our personnel policies with respect to conditions of work and payment for work such that we have a right to expect the desired level of performance from the workforce?

In smaller establishments, managers and workers are able to develop close personal relationships and a give and take situation often develops with both sides being flexible in their response to each other. Where larger numbers of people are involved, a more formal approach becomes necessary and firm data are required, based on the questions above, in order to provide management with the necessary information for them to control the operation.

If, for present purposes, we define control as the taking of effective, corrective action in the event of performance deviating from that which was planned, then, assuming that the staffing of departments is consistent with the work to be done, the first requirement is to establish plans which make clear, quantified and measurable statements of what is expected.

Some examples to illustrate possible control mechanisms useful in establishing worker performance are:

(a) indices of labour cost to sales for accommodation, food production, food service and bar operations

(b) departmental performance indices where the work in the department has been measured by means of an orthodox work measurement technique

(c) a system using records of food issued, portion control and reconciliation of issues with sales to monitor the achievement of targets for food utilisation in the case of food items which are major costs.

The calculation of departmental performance indices is fully explained in the chapter on work study under the section dealing with uses of standard times.

As with any form of control system, there is no benefit unless prompt and effective action is taken to put right the conditions which have led to any adverse results.

2.7.2 Worker attitude

In the brief list of questions requiring answers given in the section above, the question referring to the willingness of the members of the workforce to follow laid down procedures and the question mentioning personnel policies are just two of the many aspects of this most complex field of study – worker attitude. An expression of what attitude management would wish for among the workforce in the organisation would include willingness to follow legitimate orders, to give a fair day's work in return for their pay, to behave towards guests and customers in a manner likely to encourage repeat business and, perhaps, to demonstrate loyalty to their employers.

Such loyalty, however, and the response and attitudes of employees to customers and management is largely dependent on the attitudes and treatment received from customers and management. Little or nothing can be done in respect of customer treatment of employees, but the way managers deal with staff is a matter which can be considered and if necessary, varied. The responses elicited by the dictatorial, authoritarian manager are likely to be very different from those generated by the manager who is interested in consulting his staff. Much depends on precise circumstances and this topic is pursued in more detail in the next chapter.

2.8 The social responsibilities of management

In this context, social responsibilities can be defined as obligations towards various groups both within and external to the organisation. An indication of the considerations and issues to be resolved by the management of an organisation are given below under the headings of the groups of people concerned.

2.8.1 *The customers*

Do clear, unambiguous policies exist in respect of ensuring customer satisfaction? What steps are taken to ensure that employees are putting such policies into practice?

What steps, if any, are taken to establish that future plans for the sales activities of the organisation will continue to fulfil the needs and wants of prospective customers?

What is the policy regarding customer complaints and how successful does the policy appear to be?

Are customers made aware of the full cost to them of the goods and services which they are ordering (eg the inclusion or not of VAT, service charges, cover charges)?

2.8.2 *Shareholders*

What arrangements are made to keep shareholders well informed of company affairs to enable them to exercise their voting rights as owners of the company?

At what stage in planning and policy formulation are the interests of the shareholders actively considered?

2.8.3 *Employees*

Is every line manager aware of and practising company policies on employment, training, promotion, discipline and redundancy? What consultations with staff take place before the implementation of changes to work methods, procedures and other conditions which affect the staff?

What attention is given to physical working conditions, employee feeding and accommodation?

What is the prime objective of the organisation's pay policy – to attract and retain staff of high calibre or to minimise labour costs?

Does a grievance procedure exist and, if so, has it been used effectively to minimise adverse effects from conflict?

2.8.4 *Suppliers*
Are all employees whose duties bring them into contact with suppliers aware of and adhering to policy decisions on dealing with suppliers?

Are invoices settled within the time periods agreed with suppliers or is it common practice to delay settlement?

Does the ordering system allowing sufficient time for suppliers to be kept informed of changes in usage rates so that they can provide a satisfactory service?

2.8.5 *The local community*
Do policies exist which are formulated to ensure that the company is contributing to the welfare of the local community – contributions to local charities, school events and so on?

Are local interests considered when planning functions, external advertising or any other activity which affects the immediate environment?

2.8.6 *Society at large*
Is there general awareness among all levels of management of their responsibilities for the conservation of resources?

Are there regularly reviewed policies on ethical, social and environmental issues? Has any senior member of management been given the responsibility for seeing that such policies are practised?

2.8.7 *Statutory requirements*
Are all senior members of management aware of legislation relating to the conduct of business in the hotel and catering industry?

Is any named, senior manager given responsibility for keeping key people informed of legal requirements and ensuring compliance with the law?

The entries under the above seven headings are in the form of questions to indicate that these are examples of matters to be resolved by the management of that organisation, taking into account its own particular circumstances.

It can be seen that the resolution of these questions has strong moral or ethical overtones. For example, a company which makes a practice of delaying payments to suppliers until the supplying companies resort to final demands and threats of legal action may gain by working on other people's money for as long as possible. On the other hand, such a policy could lead to the development of bad relationships between buyer and supplier and in general does not lead to a satisfactory environment in which to conduct business.

The concluding passage of Robert Heller's book, *The Naked Manager*,[5] reads:

> 'Many crooks, con-men and mobsters have made great wealth. It does not follow that crookedness is the path to business success, nor that executives can throw private morality overboard as they plunge into corporate vice. Ponder, rather, how it is that the Quakers and similar deeply religious gentry made so much wordly lucre. It was because they treated their people honestly and decently, worked hard and honestly themselves, spent honestly and saved pennies, honestly put back into the company more than they took out, made honestly good products, gave honest value for money and, being honest, told no lies.'

3 CONSTRAINTS ON OBJECTIVES SETTING

It has already been stated that objectives should be attainable. To set objectives at an unrealistic level is counter-productive, because as soon as staff realise that the objective is not likely to be achieved, they 'switch off' and positive motivation is completely lost. Reasons why objectives might not be attainable could lie in the inability or lack of training of employees ie, they might not have the requisite skills; alternatively the physical and financial resources may not be adequate – the plant may not be able to cope with the required output, the money may not be available for an advertising campaign; sufficient numbers of staff might not be available; the required raw materials might be too expensive to make the exercise profitable and so on.

Apart from these constraints, other limiting factors must be considered. Most companies lay down certain policies within which their employees must operate. Policies may be defined as guides for making administrative decisions, or as administrative laws governing administrative actions and which guide or channel thinking in the making of decisions. In short, policies become formalised ways of doing things, and consequently limit the scope for individual discretion. There is an inherent inconsistency in giving, say, the person responsible for purchasing the requirement to buy supplies 'as economically as possible, consistent with quality' and at the same time limiting his suppliers to three and instructing that goods can only be purchased from one or more of the nominated suppliers.

In formulating objectives and communicating objectives to employees therefore, it is essential that any constraints which might influence the objectives setting process are taken into account at the outset.

4 SUMMARY

In discussing the role of Objectives and Objectives Setting we have concentrated in this chapter on those which relate to the company as a whole and which are intended to determine what is to be done and where the company is intending to go. Objectives are thus directional, and identify a point to be reached or achieved.

It will be apparent that objectives need to be communicated to individuals at all levels of the organisation. Managers and staff need to be made aware of their responsibilities and one means of doing this is discussed in the next chapter – Management by Objectives.

References

[1] MASSIE, J L and DOUGLAS, J, *Managing a Contemporary Introduction*, p 217, Prentice Hall, Englewood, New Jersey. 1973

[2] DRUCKER, P F, *The Practice of Management*, p 66-112, Pan Books, London SW1, 1971

[3] DOSWELL, R, *Towards an Integrated Approach to Hotel Planning*, New University Education, Central Press, Aberdeen, 1970

[4] KOTAS, R, *Market Orientation in the Hotel and Catering Industry*, chapter 3, Surrey University Press, 1975

[5] HELLER, R, *The Naked Manager*, Barrie and Jenkins, London, 1972

3
Management
by objectives

1 THE PURPOSE AND AIMS OF MANAGEMENT BY OBJECTIVES (MBO)

MBO is an approach to management which is concerned with human behaviour and motivation at all levels of management, and which involves people in helping to set their own targets or objectives, rather than having them imposed by a superior. The involvement of people in the establishment of their individual objectives leads to personal commitment to their achievement and, as a result, to them becoming self-motivated rather than needing control by their superior. Instead of superiors constantly telling their subordinates what to do, when and how to do it, subordinates accept responsibility for the achievement of certain goals or the completion of specific tasks often on the basis of exercising their own judgement and discretion as to the specific method to be used.

This approach is an invaluable method of helping an individual to develop his skills, as, under the guidance of his superior, he is able to learn through doing.

As has already been stressed, objectives need to be stated in terms which make it possible to determine, without undue difficulty, the amount of progress being made towards them. It might, for example, be agreed by the manager of an individual hotel in a group that one of his objectives for the coming year is to raise the occupancy ratio from say, 70% to 85% as an average for the year, or that for the months of March and April it should be raised from 60% to 75%. Having agreed this target with his superior at Head Office his determination to actually achieve what he has said he can achieve will be that much greater – self motivation and self-control come into play.

It is evident that not only is it necessary to know what is to be achieved, ie what the objectives are, but also that people should be made aware of the progress (or lack of it) they are making.

It is an essential of MBO that such control information is made available on a regular, ongoing basis. Then, individuals can compare their actual performance with projected performance and institute corrective action where necessary. It is this self-evaluation and self-control which is the key to effective MBO, and which is so important in staff motivation.

Figure 2   The cycle of Management by Objectives ▷

2 THE OPERATION OF MANAGEMENT BY OBJECTIVES

MBO is best viewed as a cycle, or ongoing sequence of events, each of which will be examined separately. (See figure 2.)

2.1 Company objectives

It has already been stated (chapter 2) that the responsibility for the formulation of objectives for the company as a whole lies with top management, be it board of directors, the management committee or the owner. Only when such overall objectives have been stated, clearly and precisely, can MBO be brought into effective operation. The mere statement of objectives is not sufficient in itself, but requires a suitable organisation (Box 1).

2.2 Company organisation

As the means of achieving objectives, duties are assigned to individuals who are responsible for their being discharged properly. This process is known as Delegation, and the assignment of duties is the means by which an organisation structure is created, usually through the departmentalisation of activities eg the appointment of managers to be responsible for Food and Beverage Accommodation, Marketing, Personnel and so on. Each of these managers will agree with his superior (the general manager) exactly what he or she is responsible for. The structure so created, should be that which is most appropriate to the objectives. It should also be noted that organisations are not static frameworks, but are dynamic and subject to change as circumstances require (Box 2).

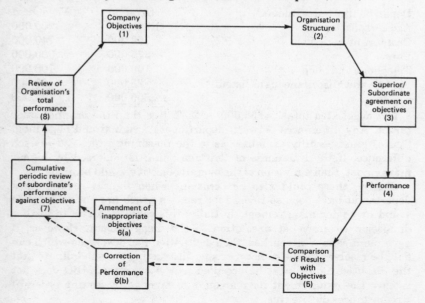

31

2.3 Superior/Subordinate agreement on objectives

The main point about MBO is that it involves agreement about objectives between a superior and his subordinates. Targets are agreed not imposed. Subordinates are thus participating in the setting of their own targets, and negotiation is involved. There will be some tension involved until trust is established.

Usually, subordinates tend to be cautious and try to negotiate objectives at a fairly easily attainable level. By so doing they feel there is less chance of failure and consequent loss of face. Conversely, superiors may attempt to set objectives too high, as a means of insuring against limited short fall in performance.

There is no set procedure for resolving such divergencies, it is a matter of limited compromise between the two parties, but once agreed, subordinates are motivated by the personally felt need to achieve that which they have said they can achieve.

The process of objective setting then proceeds at successively lower levels in the organisation.

If true agreement on objectives is to be attained in the negotiating process, then it is more than likely that revisions will be necessary to the figures at various stages in those negotiations. It is also necessary to reconcile the total of all departmental objectives, in terms of sales targets and cost constraints, with the overall objectives for the whole organisation.

Example

Total Sales Budget for the year: *£2,500,000*

Departmental Sales Budgets :	Original	Negotiated
Accommodation	1,250,000	1,200,000
Restaurant	750,000	740,000
Bars	375,000	380,000
Telephone and Shop	100,000	100,000
Rentals and Miscellaneous as listed	25,000	25,000
	£2,500,000	£2,445,000

The negotiated total is £55,000 or 2.2% less than the original sales target. Any differences between departmental original and negotiated figures must be fully explained as to the reasoning which led to each difference. If the soundness of that reasoning is endorsed by higher mangement, then a revision of the overall objective would be made.

Clearly, there could also be occasions when figures revised by a department have been so revised for reasons which are not accepted as sound by senior management. Initially, this could give rise to further discussion to arrive at a solution to the disagreement. However, if agreement cannot be reached, then a situation has developed which can only be resolved by the senior manager instructing the subordinate that the disputed figure must be accepted as the objective. MBO does not remove the requirement for managers to manage by issuing orders if circumstances dictate this.

The Food and Beverage Manager will now, having agreed his objectives, be able to discuss with his subordinates, his Restaurant Managers, Bar Managers and Head Chef, exactly what they are to achieve as contributions to the achievement of the objectives he has agreed with his superior (Box 3).

2.4 Performance

Staff now have agreed their own objectives and know what it is they have to do. Effective performance requires that they are provided with the necessary resources, training and guidance for the efficient execution of their duties. They know the objectives they have agreed, and need ongoing information as to their progress. Whether objectives lie in the field of achieving sales, reducing expenses, portion control or yields from raw materials, information as to performance is vital, and must be provided as soon as possible and regularly (Box 4).

2.5 Comparison of results with objectives

The manager seeking to increase his occupancy ratio from 70% to 85% for the year cannot wait until November to learn that the average being achieved is only 75%. He needs to know on a daily, weekly or monthly basis the actual occupancy achieved. Only when armed with such information can remedial action be taken (Box 5).

Divergence from objectives may be dealt with in two ways. Either it may be necessary to amend objectives which experience shows are inappropriate (either too high or too low) or, it may be that it is the performance of the individual which needs improvement (Boxes 6a and 6b).

2.6 Cumulative periodic review of subordinate's performance against objectives

Reviews of performance should be ongoing and not just an annual occurrence. Information as to performance should be provided on a regular basis, daily, weekly etc. as appropriate, and also on a cumulative basis. Comparison can then be made with targets prepared in the same way, and this reconciliation of budgetted results with targets is an ongoing process.

To use a simple example concerning sales:

| Week ending | SALES | | | | | |
| | Budget | | Actual | | Variance | |
	Weekly	Cumulative	Weekly	Cumulative	Weekly	Cumulative
Jan 7	10,000		9,300		− 700	
Jan 14	10,300	20,300	10,100	19,400	− 200	− 900
Jan 21	10,400	30,700	10,550	29,950	+ 150	− 750
Jan 28	10,600	41,300	10,000	39,950	− 600	− 1350

The use of statistical information clearly shows the performance of an individual or department in weekly and cumulative terms and facilitates analysis of the variances and an investigation of causes (Box 7).

2.7 Review of company's total performance

Application of MBO inevitably means that individual's own performance will be appraised as indicated above. Beyond the evaluation of individual performance lies that of the organisation as a whole. Total results in relation to objectives need to be assessed, not just for the purpose of seeing how close actual performance come to objectives, but also to determine how the organisation helped to achieve, or alternatively hindered, the attainment of objectives.

This review is important whether or not objectives have been achieved. If targets have been reached, it may simply mean that they have been set at too low a level. External factors may have intervened to improve or impair performance. A rail strike might fill city-centre hotels or a sudden increase in the value of the pound may significantly reduce the number of foreign visitors to this country. Such events are outside the control of the organisation, but do need be be considered during the review process.

The sort of questions which should be asked during this process include:
Does the present organisation help or hinder the achievement of results?
Are resources (of all types) adequate?
Were the targets realistic?
What changes might be made before embarking on the next cycle? (Box 8).

3 THE BENEFITS OF MANAGEMENT BY OBJECTIVES

Properly installed MBO helps management in the following ways:
- the objectives of the firm are examined and made explicit
- detailed plans and objectives derive from general objectives
- individuals know exactly what they have agreed to do
- communications between superior and subordinates improve
- the control system improves through the evaluation process
- training needs can be identified
- self-motivation is encouraged
- staff come to understand how their personal efforts contribute to the company's objectives
- problems affecting performance can more easily identified
- manpower planning can be improved.

4 SOME LIMITATIONS OF MBO

The system of MBO is not a magic remedy for all organisational ills. If essential features of the system are neglected, then more harm than good could be the result. The following points summarise both the essential features and certain aspects of management behaviour which could limit, or even eliminate the assistance which MBO can offer a user organisation.

a) If management at the highest level do not participate fully in the application of the system, it will fail.
(b) In the case of an organisation suffering from bad relationships between superior and subordinate managers, then MBO of itself is unlikely to improve those relationships.
(c) Any organisation which is basically unsound, which has managers lacking in competence and has goods and services which are not viable market propositions is most unlikely to benefit from MBO.
(d) The training of managers in analysing job situations and all other factors relevant to setting objectives, in evaluating performances and carrying out appraisal interviews with subordinates is a lengthy and expensive procedure. Yet it is fatal to skimp this training.
(e) In evaluating performances it is obviously necessary to make allowances for under-achievement which is due to external factors beyond the control of the job-holder. Yet if mere excuses rather than real reasons are accepted in the case of poor performances, the whole system could be seriously weakened.
(f) Any system which allows one person to evaluate the performance of another in complex areas which may be open to different interpretations, must have some form of grievance procedure. The agreement of a grievance procedure in the circumstances of MBO can be very difficult. Additionally, a poorly designed procedure could damage relationships between managers at different levels.
(g) MBO also focuses on individual performance whereas in many situations it is the team effort which is important rather than that of the individual, and to that end more emphasis might be placed on agreeing objectives for groups of people who will develop a common purpose and will readily help each other.

5 MANAGEMENT STYLES MOTIVATION AND MBO
5.1 Management styles
A number of different styles of management have been identified and LIKERT[1] for example suggests that there are four main systems:
1 The exploitive-authoritative system where decisions are imposed on subordinates, where motivation is characterised by threats, where high levels of management have great responsibilities but lower levels have virtually none, where there is very little communication and joint teamwork.
2 The benevolent-authoritative system where leadership is by a condescending form of master-servant trust, where motivation is mainly by rewards, where managerial personnel feel responsibility but lower levels do not, where there is little communication and relatively little teamwork.
3 The consultative system where leadership is by superiors who have substantial but not complete trust in their subordinates, where motivation is by reward and some involvement, where a high proportion of personnel, especially those at the higher levels feel

responsibility for achieving organisational goals, where there is some communication (both vertical and horizontal) and a moderate amount of teamwork.

4   The participative-group system which is the optimum solution, where leadership is by superiors who have complete confidence in their subordinates, where motivation is by economic rewards based on goals which have been set in participation, where personnel at all levels feel real responsibility for the organisational goals, where there is much communication, and a substantial amount of co-operative teamwork.

MICHAEL WHITE[2], assistant director of research at Ashridge Management College also identified four management styles and looked at their success in hotels:

Four styles of management
Manager A: Makes his decision promptly and communicates it to his subordinates clearly and firmly. He expects them to carry it out loyally and without raising difficulties.
Manager B: Makes his decision promptly, but then tries to get his subordinates' agreement to it before going ahead. He believes in carrying his staff with him rather than issuing orders.
Manager C: Does not reach his decision until he has consulted his subordinates. He listens to their advice, weighs it and then announces his decision. He then expects all to work loyally to implement it irrespective of whether or not it is in accordance with the advice they gave.
Manager D: Calls a meeting of his staff whenever there is an important decision to take. He lays the problem before the group and invites discussion. He accepts the majority viewpoint as the decision.

These are the descriptions used to define the four management styles discussed in the article.
Manager A = 'autocratic'
Manager B = 'persuasive'
Manager C = 'consultative'
Manager D = 'participative'

He found that the majority of employees saw their boss as of the autocratic style, and that this style is much more evident in hotels than in manufacturing industry. His research also showed that the majority of hotel employees accepted a strict disciplinarian approach, but that they would prefer a more consultative style. Those less than thirty years of age were much less willing to accept the strict approach.

There can be no one style of management appropriate to all circumstances. The hotel and catering industry is characterised by a high labour turn-over, especially at the lower levels of the organisation. The presence of short service staff, often unskilled, is no incentive to management to introduce a consultative approach to management. At more senior levels consultation and discussion between, say, departmental heads about immediate and long-term objectives is a common approach to management.

Other factors also influence the choice of managerial style. Skilled employees, the head chef, for example, should need little direct supervision and control, whereas those with little or no skill will usually need to be closely supervised. Different circumstances will influence the immediate selection of managerial approach.

Faced with an emergency the manager who is normally participative in his approach will become autocratic and authoritarian until the crisis has passed. There may well be a difference in approach of an owner manager of a small hotel and management in, say, the National Health Service or a works canteen where employees are members of a Trade Union.

Although different management styles can be identified, no one style can be said to be the right one; much depends on the nature and size of the organisation and the specific group of people being directed.

As far as individual managers are concerned, personality differences will lead to different approaches; the styles are not mutually exclusive, but adaptable and interchangeable to meet different circumstances.

5.2 Motivation

One of the principle benefits of MBO is the personal motivation of the individuals involved. Through participating in the setting of objectives and subsequently through their achievement, they feel a sense of personal accomplishment. They feel that what they do is important and consequently it is rewarding to them. This is further re-inforced if they are accorded praise for the work they have done.

Fear or the use of threats to coerce people into working is seen by some as an effective motivation. Punishment, or the ultimate threat of dismissal may be effective but is usually considered to be less effective than other means such as participation and the encouragement of the individual.

There are a number of theories as to which approach to human motivation generates the desired performance. Space prevents an examination of them here, but those interested should refer to the work of McGregor[3], Herzberg[4] and Maslow[5].

6 SUMMARY

In conclusion, MBO is defined in HM Treasury's *Glossary of Management Techniques*[6] as follows:

'a technique under which targets are fixed on a basis for achieving greater effectiveness throughout the whole of an organisation or part of an organisation. The system involves the fixing of agreed and realistic targets for an organisation (or part of it) in precise quantitative terms, eg to increase the output of work by x per cent, to reduce the time taken over a process by y per cent, or to reduce the error rate by z per cent. The factors which impede the attainment of these objectives are then identified and courses of action, including training, are agreed in order to remove them. The results achieved are periodically appraised and new targets set. It is important that individual targets are not only clear and realistic in

themselves, but also that each should contribute effectively to the aims of the organisation. The approach is based on the view that targets agreed by a manager and his subordinates are in themselves an incentive and that they form a yardstick against which performance can be measured'.
This statement summarizes the situation perfectly.

References

1   LIKERT, R, *Human Organisation; Its Management and Value,* McGraw-Hill, 1967
2   WHITE, M, *Management Styles in Hotels,* p 9, HCIMA Journal, October 1973
3   McGREGOR, D, *The Human Side of the Enterprise,* McGraw-Hill, New York, 1960
4   HERZBERG, F, *The Motivation-Hygiene Concept and Problems in Manpower,* Personnel Administration Jan-Feb 1964
5   MASLOW, A H, 'A Theory of Human Motivation' in *Psychological Review,* Vol 50, 1943, pp 370-396
6   HM TREASURY Glossary of Management Techniques, Extract reproduced with the permission of the Controller of Her Majesty's Stationery Office. HMSO London, 1969.

4
Planning

1 THE NEED FOR PLANNING

Planning is concerned with looking at the future and identifying alternative courses of action. Plans are derived from objectives and concerned with the way in which objectives are to be achieved. In chapters 2 and 3 we examined the nature of organisational objectives, the areas in which objectives should be set and the formulation of departmental and individual objectives.

The fact that objectives have been set, or agreed, in no way guarantees their achievement. Plans are the means by which objectives are to be achieved. KOONTZ and O'DONNELL[1] liken plans to a bridge, and the concept of a plan as a bridge is useful, as one can visualise a plan as the means of getting from the present situation to the intended future situation.

A plan should structure behaviour and performance in a sensible, coherent way. The alternative to a planned approach is random uncontrolled behaviour.

Activities at all levels of an organisation require to be planned. The objective of opening ten new units over the next ten years will not be achieved unless the venture is planned; an extension to increase accommodation must be planned; re-decoration or re-equipping need to be planned to minimise inconvenience.

A restaurant in which specific groups of tables were not allocated to individual waiters or waitresses would not operate very effectively. It is the job of the Restaurant Manager, or Head Waiter to determine who will serve which tables. Such planning is necessary to enable the Head Waiter to achieve his objective of a well-run restaurant. His efforts alone, of course, will not guarantee this, because he is dependent on the efficiency of kitchen staff in ensuring that the food is properly cooked and made available for service at the right time.

Liaison between departments is therefore necessary. No department or section of an organisation can be treated in isolation or operate in isolation, since decisions and plans made in one will inevitably affect the other. What happens in the restaurant influences activities in the kitchen and vice versa, to use but a simple example. Similar considerations apply to all departments and to avoid (as far as possible) crises and dislocations to service, means of communication between managers and staff and between departments must be developed, as must the mechanics of co-ordinating related activities.

Planning therefore, it not an activity just for top management, it is something involving every employee in order to avoid inefficiency, delay and waste. Some will plan their activities in advance (often in order to minimise effort) others will need help and training to enable them to plan their work effectively. This is one of the responsibilities of management – to plan the training, where necessary, of their subordinates.

2 INFORMATION NEEDS

Objective setting requires information; plans can only be drawn up when an adequate data base is available to allow managers to evaluate the various possible courses of action open to them.

A decision (plan) to open a new hotel or restaurant in a neighbouring town would not be sensible without first seeking information as to the type of consumer in the locality, their preferences, the type and level of competition, the price levels in the area and the availability of suitable staff to manage and run the new unit. Even before reaching this stage, the availability of the necessary funds for the project would need to be established.

The efficient internal operation of a unit is also heavily dependent on the availability of information, which needs to be gathered and analysed as an ongoing activity. Management needs sales and profit figures analysed according to the various services supplied. Information about sales of meals in the restaurant analysed by each item on the menu, whether sold at lunch or dinner and on which day is required. Such information can easily be obtained from restaurant bills – it simply requires extracting, and if this is done on a regular basis, will indicate trends over time.

Similarly, reservations for accommodation can be analysed to identify sources of business; if you know where your existing clientele is coming from, then you can deduce the potential clientele you are not currently attracting, and use this as the basis for planning a promotional campaign to influence them.

Much information is available in a company's own internal accounting/ records systems. More can be obtained by the relatively simple expedient of management talking to guests and seeking their opinions of quality and service. Short questionnaires placed in bedrooms are another simple way of obtaining information.

A comprehensive exposition of the range of information needed for planning is to be found in AXLER[2] to which those seeking more detailed information can refer.

3 FORECASTING

Information available about the various areas of operation of an organisation is always historic and, consequently, out of date. Knowing, for example, the prices of all cuts and types of meat two years ago is of little use in trying to estimate the cost in say, three months time. If, however, the data has been recorded on a weekly basis for the past two years, then changes and trends can be detected and reasonable predictions made.

Occupancy figures recorded over the years enable seasonal patterns to be identified and indicate the appropriate time to plan an advertising campaign. In a restaurant, the cycle is much shorter and the pattern of meals sold may reveal itself in three of four weeks.

Knowledge of past performance provides the basis for estimating future activity and planning future operations, but it is only a basis. Were events to continually repeat themselves there would be little need for planning, as we would always know exactly what to do. In reality, of course, circumstances are rarely the same, and the demand for our products and services will vary according to the weather, the economic situation, the level of unemployment, transport difficulties, competitors activities and so on. Sensible forecasting takes account of these factors and makes suitable adjustments.

4 DECISION MAKING

Having gathered the necessary information on which to base forecasts, it becomes necessary for management to consider the range of possible choices and to decide which one is the best in the circumstances. Management is about making choices – the best choices. In most situations there are a number of possible courses of action, but rarely a situation where there is only one 'right' choice. Objectives may be reached in a number of ways, and the way *Manager A* chooses may not be the way *Manager B* would have chosen, but each could be as effective as the other.

Choices and decisions are influenced by management's interpretation of the circumstances affecting the operating situation and in its turn this interpretation is influenced by past education and experience. A manager must decide which information is important in relation to his objectives – is it more important that he should use only fresh vegetables of top quality or will tinned or frozen varieties be acceptable? – is quality more important than price? – should an item on the menu be withdrawn because its present cost would eliminate profit, or should it be offered and the menu price increased, or should it be offered at the existing price and the loss absorbed in the interests of goodwill?

These, and similar choices face management constantly. When information has been accumulated and choices made, then plans can be prepared to show the way in which objectives are to be realised.

5 TYPES OF PLAN

In very broad terms, plans can be separated into those which are intended to be long-standing in their use and application, and those which are designed to achieve a particular objective within a defined time-scale.

5.1 Long-standing plans

In any organisation there are many situations which occur with a degree of regularity. It is not necessary that management should consider each of these situations each time it occurs but that prescribed methods of dealing with them as they arise are developed.

5.1.1 *Policies*

Policies are the result of careful decision making and are guides to management activities in all sectors of the business. A company seeking to serve a high-class market could well decide that only foodstuffs of the highest quality would be used in the kitchen. This decision, once taken, would be established as a policy – the policy to buy nothing but the best raw materials does not need a fresh decision to be taken each time an order is placed. Similarly a policy decision might be made to promote from within wherever possible, or to advertise the unit in the local paper every week.

Such simple examples illustrate the point that, once established, policies guide the action to be taken in a particular situation.

Policies usually allow the exercise of some discretion, and allow some flexibility. For example the policy of advertising every week might be adjusted to, say, a fortnightly or monthly advertisement if customer demand rose to, and remained at, an extremely high level.

5.1.2 *Procedures*

Procedures are more restrictive than policies and lay down precisely the way in which certain activities are to be carried out. Hotels will have established procedures and systems for dealing with reservations, all of which will be processed in the same way, and staff will be trained to follow the same procedural steps to minimise the chance of error. A company might decide to adopt a policy of preventitive maintenance for all its equipment. Procedures would then be written detailing precisely the step by step actions which are required for each piece of equipment.

It is for management to decide what procedures are necessary and appropriate to its own department.

5.1.3 *Rules*

Rules are more precise than either Policies or Procedures and state exactly what must, or must not be done in specific circumstances. 'No Smoking in the Kitchen' is an example of a rule; it is not a guide to action or a way of proceeding, but a clear indication of behaviour which is not permitted. Rules cover items like the time at which employees are to report for work, the penalties for late arrival, holiday entitlement, the covering of hair in the kitchen, for example. No discretion is allowed and normally penalties for non-compliance are exacted.

5.2 Single-purpose plans

In contrast to Policies, Procedures and Rules, which are designed to deal with recurring situations, single purpose plans are the means of achieving a particular objective within a specific time scale.

Budgets for sales, production expenses, personnel, costs and profit are examples of such plans and their purpose is to guide and influence operations during the currency of the budget (plan). Each of the plans is prepared for the purpose of achieving one particular objective, and collectively these objectives should constitute the overall objectives of the organisation.

One of the main tasks of senior managers is to co-ordinate and unify the activities being carried on under these various detailed plans so that progress towards the main objective is maintained.

6 THE TIME DIMENSION OF PLANNING

Plans may be classified according to the time-scale envisaged for their completion on a short-term/long-term continuum. Such descriptions are, however, relative and what is short-term in one context may be long-term in another.

Plans to increase sales in the next three or six months may be viewed as a short-term activity by the marketing manager; a head-chef however sees the situation to be planned for in the next few hours as his short-term and a banquet planned for a fortnight hence is long-term in his eyes. In the previously quoted example of a company planning to open two new restaurants a year for the next five years the plans for the fifth year will be viewed by the managing director as long-term and next year's projected activities as short-term.

A broad relationship exists between levels in the organisation and the time scale of the plans with which individuals at each level of the organisation are involved.

The senior levels of management are mainly concerned with yearly plans and strategies in activities such as sales and volume objectives. Middle management is usually concerned with the execution of the strategic plans – perhaps on the basis of monthly or quarterly plans.

At the more junior levels of management the principal concern is with day-to-day or even hour-to-hour planning and operation.

It should not be assumed that senior managers are concerned solely with distant future planning, but that the bulk of their planning activities are so focussed. They do of course, have concern for immediate situations and how they should be dealt with, but this occupies far less of their time. Correspondingly junior management will normally have only limited involvement in long-term planning in contrast with more immediate planning involvements.

Plans made at senior management level tend to be broad in concept and stated in very general terms. A sales director's objective of 'maximising profitable sales volume' might result in a sales budget being agreed for each of the sectors he controls, and at each succeeding subordinate level plans become more detailed until at the lowest level of activity the plans to be executed are extremely detailed.

7 FACTORS AFFECTING PLANNING

Planning is concerned with making decisions as to what is to be achieved, by whom and when the results are expected.

Two extremes can be identified, first that plans are formulated and imposed on subordinates and secondly the management by objectives approach (dealt with in chapter 3) where subordinates are involved in setting their own objectives. At either extreme, or in any intermediate position chosen, management needs to take into account the following:

7.1 Information
Plans can only be properly prepared given an adequate information base. The key to planning is to reduce to an absolute minimum guesswork and assumptions underlying the plans. It is never possible to have all the information one would like, partly because the cost of compilation might be too high and also because the time required for its collection might not be available. Nevertheless the more information one has, the more accurately one can plan.

7.2 Communication
Plans result from the choices and decisions made by management, and as has been previously indicated in this chapter, decisions are made on the basis of information. The gathering and transmission of the required data involves a process of communication to get the required information to the person at the point of decision. It will be apparent that it is also necessary to inform those concerned of the plans which have been made and of the decisions which have been taken. As activities are undertaken, so can comparisons be made between actual and planned performance. The results of such comparison must be communicated to those needing the information.

Such communication will normally be in writing, taking the form of letters, memos, notices, reports, job descriptions etc. In a rapidly changing situation, say in a kitchen, then all communication might be verbal.

This brief comment is intended only to emphasize the need for and the importance of the communication process and the fact that inadequate information flows may impair the quality of the plans in the initial stages and also prevent the timely operational adjustments which might be called for.

Communication is dealt with more fully in chapter 6.

7.3 Human Obstacles
One of the difficulties connected with planning is that those involved tend to be prisoners of their own past, and to make plans based on their previously accumulated experience. As long as their experience has relevance to the present situation, this may cause few problems. If, however, there is no such match, difficulties may ensue and it may be necessary to include within the planning circle, those with suitable experience and inspiration to cope with the situation.

A second problem arises from people's attitudes to their jobs and the way they have become accustomed to carrying out their daily tasks. We tend to be conservative in our approach, and reluctant to change. For most of us, the *status quo* is attractive. By their nature, plans usually involve change and require people to act differently. In consequence there is a tendency for such changes to be viewed from entrenched positions, and for them to be resisted. A change from a silver-service type of restaurant operation to say a fast food or cold-buffet may meet with resistance from staff who have spent years in the former situation.

Dealing with this type of problem requires understanding on the part of management, and a recognition of the need to explain the proposed changes (communication) and to motivate staff to understand the reasons for the changes, to accept them and to implement them enthusiastically.

8 EVALUATION OF PERFORMANCE AGAINST PLANS

It is not proposed to deal with this topic in depth here, since it forms the substance of chapter 7 on Control. We have said that plans derive from objectives and represent the way in which those objectives are to be realised. Plans thus require the attainment of specific targets which must initially be communicated to those responsible for their attainment. Actual performance must then be measured, compared with the target and variances (if any) established. The causes of any variations must be established and remedial action taken where appropriate either in terms of individual performance, or in respect the plans themselves.

It will be appreciated that in arriving at budgeted sales targets as in section 2.6 of chapter 3, the means of control is also established. The preparation of the budget is a planning exercise which also provides a control mechanism.

9 THE DYNAMIC NATURE OF PLANNING

The nature of the internal and external environments in which management operates has been considered at some length in Chapter 1, in which numerous examples were cited of the factors which influence management. These factors affect the objectives which are agreed upon and consequently also affect the plans which are made to achieve the objectives.

Planning is therefore not an activity which can be undertaken without due consideration being given to those internal and external influences which are constantly changing. The loss of skilled staff in any part of the hotel and the management of others less skilled and needing training may necessitate the modification of plans as may increases in the cost of materials and power; a change in the rate of VAT may require sales budgets for accommodation or the restaurant to be revised, as may the opening of a new hotel or restaurant within the current catchment area of the unit.

10 PLANNING FLEXIBILITY

The consequence of the foregoing comments is that plans and planning require a flexible approach and recognition that plans must be subject to modification. Plans are not to be regarded as sacrosanct and immutable but as subject to modification and amendment as and when changing circumstances indicate the need. Should it be deemed necessary to change a plan early in the period to which it applies, then probably the better approach is to change the plan and calculate fresh targets or budgets. Should the need for change become apparent late in the life of the plan then it might be preferable to let existing targets stand and simply note the variances which occur and provide suitable explanations and comments.

Two cautionary points should be noted. First, care should be taken not to change plans in haste before the circumstances which indicate the need to do so can be seen as long-term and not a purely temporary fluctuation. Secondly, it is essential for management to keep itself fully informed and aware of both the internal and external environments and the changes and trends therein.

11 SUMMARY

Planning is concerned with the clarification of the end-results which are required and the establishment of criteria against which performance can be measured so that everyone in the organisation knows what is expected of them. It is concerned with the disposition of duties to departments and individuals, and with the co-ordination of such duties and of the relevant resources.

Properly executed, planning encourages consistent action rather than ad hoc responses to problems and assists in the early identification of problems, leading to the development of possible solutions and the projection of future activities in the light of the information available at the time.

In essence, planning requires an accurate analysis of all available resources, knowledge of past performance, an assessment of the current situation and clearly formulated objectives.

References

[1]   KOONTZ and O'DONNELL, *Principles of Management: An Analysis of Managerial Functions,* McGraw-Hill, New York 1968/81

[2]   AXLER, B H, *Foodservice: A Managerial Approach,* D C Heath and Company, National Institute for the Food Service Industry 1979.

5
Organisation

1 ORGANISATION AND PLANNING

We have seen that in order to reach objectives, it is necessary to make plans. The making of plans and making of decisions as to which departments, sections and individuals are to be accountable for which activities, is the first step in the organising process. In deciding who is to do what, the chief executive, whatever his title, is creating an organisation structure.

The decisions as to the activities needed to fulfil the plans and objectives and as to the groupings of the activities thus designated into appropriate departments should create a logical framework or structure. Positions of specific responsibility are identified and to them is allocated the requisite authority to enable the individuals concerned to achieve their objectives.

Complexity of organisation is a function of size, and the larger the organisation, the more complex it is likely to be. The term 'organisation' is often used synonymously with company, business or enterprise and does give an impression of a large scale operation, but large size is not a prerequisite, and if two people decide to open a small cafe, for example, an organisation comes into being.

They will have an objective, probably to make a living for themselves and will make plans and decisions accordingly. They will decide, perhaps that one should be responsible for purchasing and production, the other to take on the selling/service side of the business. Thus size itself is not a criterion for deciding what constitutes an organisation; an organisation comes into being when people decide to work together and to carry out a plan as a means of achieving an objective. In a large hotel, the numbers of staff may be high and the number of levels in an organisation may be many.

There will be a range of job-titles and activities to be arranged into a coherent structure, ranging from General Manager, Deputy General Manager, Assistant Manager, Head Chef, Restaurant Manager, Room Service Manager, Head Waiter, Chef de Rang and so on. The ideal in arranging all the parts, is to do so in such a way that the whole structure works with the greatest efficiency to execute the plans which have been prepared for the achievement of the corporate objective/s. This requires people to appreciate the nature of the overall objectives, the action they need to contribute as individuals and their willingness to co-operate with other employees in the organisation.

2 THE ORGANISING PROCESS

The organising process can be demonstrated as a logical sequence of steps which could equally apply to the setting up of a new enterprize, or to a review of an existing situation with a view to its possible improvement.

The first step is to formulate or redefine the overall objectives of the enterprize, so that those involved in subsequent stages can be aware of the goals towards which their individual activities are to be directed.

Next, departmental or secondary objectives and the policies and plans necessary for the realisation of the overall objectives must be formulated.

Thirdly, all the activities or jobs necessary to carry out the plans properly must be listed, classified and then formed into the groups most appropriate to the human and material resources available.

Fourthly, the person in charge of each group must have delegated to him the necessary authority to enable him to carry out his duties effectively.

Finally, the various groups which have been formed must be linked together both horizontally and vertically into authority relationships and communication networks which can be represented in an organisation chart, the use of which is discussed in section 4 of this chapter.

3 DELEGATION

Delegation is the action of a superior giving to a subordinate the authority to carry out work which the superior could have retained and done himself.

This action involves three important concepts:

3.1 Responsibility

In the context of delegation, the work, or duties or tasks allocated to the subordinate are referred to as the 'responsibility' which is delegated to him.

3.2 Authority

This is the power, or right given to a subordinate to enable him to carry out effectively the responsibilities delegated to him. The nature of this authority will vary according to the nature of the responsibilities delegated, but might include, for example the right to engage staff, to purchase goods and equipment, to place advertisements in the press and so on. It would also include the right to give instructions to any subordinates the delegatee might have, and also to delegate to his subordinates such parts of his responsibilities as he chooses.

3.3 Accountability

To be accountable means that an individual is held to account for the way in which he has discharged the responsibilities delegated to him, and that he is answerable to his superior (delegator) for the success or failure achieved in carrying out his duties. This does not mean that a manager can divest himself of his accountability to his superior for everything that happens in his department. His accountability is still total, even though he might not be aware of all decisions and actions taken by the subordinates to whom he has delegated certain responsibilities. The General Manager is accountable to the Board for *all* the actions of his Departmental Managers. The Food and Beverage Manager is accountable to the General Manager for the actions and decisions of his Restaurant Manager/s, the Head Waiter, the Head Chef and Bar Managers. They, in their turn, are of course accountable to the Restaurant Manager, but this does not diminish his accountability to the General Manager for their activities.

Successful delegation requires that the responsibilities assigned to individuals be matched by the authority given to them. If people do not have sufficient power or authority to enable them to give the necessary instructions, order the required goods, or hire the necessary staff, then delegation has not been properly carried out and inefficiency will be the result. The assignment of such authority does involve the taking of calculated risks and therefore requires great care in the selection of the staff chosen to carry out the responsibilities delegated to them.

3.4 The practice of delegation

There are certain basic rules to be borne in mind when delegation is practised:

1   It is a job or task which is being delegated, not the delegator's accountability to his superior, which remains however much he chooses to delegate.
2   Where responsibility and authority are delegated, the nature and extent of the delegation must be made clear to both the delegatee and to those over whom he will exercise the authority he has been given.
3   Once delegation has taken place, the delegatee should be left to get on with the job with the minimum interference.
4   It will be necessary for periodic checks on performance to be made during which the subordinate should be given the chance to express his opinions about the way the job is going. Where a subordinate has discharged his responsibilities well, he should be congratulated.
5   Delegation is not permanent and jobs which have been assigned to subordinate may be recovered or modified at the discretion of the superior.

3.5 Benefits of delegation

The need for delegation arises simply because it is not possible for one person to do everything and consequently needs to assign tasks to others. Moreover, the complex nature of business operations requires the services of specialists in such fields as Finance, Personnel, Marketing, Food and Beverage Management, Accommodation, etc. There is also a need for staff to be trained.

The benefits of delegation include:

1   the delegator is able to concentrate on those things he does best, and to delegate those he does less well

2   the benefits of specialisation are increased in that people are enabled to concentrate on those things they do best
3   specialisation tends to improve staff morale because they become more interested in doing the work they prefer, are enabled to exercise some initiative and thereby become more confident
4   the training element is important in that staff, by assuming greater responsibilities, develop confidence in themselves and their capabilities for further promotion
5   the performance of subordinates is more easily controlled and monitored when their responsibilities have been defined and explained clearly, and accepted by the subordinate.

3.6 Difficulties of delegation
The difficulties associated with delegation are often more apparent than real, but include:
1   the fear that the subordinate will not perform well. This can be overcome by careful planning, clear explanation of what is involved and by showing faith and confidence in the delegatee
2   the difficulty of assigning a task which a superior enjoys and does well to a subordinate
3   some managers feel that they lose control and get 'out of touch' when they delegate. Additionally there is the fear that the delegatee will 'not do the job as well as I do'. This may well be true initially, but with training and the opportunity to grow into the job, provided the person chosen has the capacity, this should only be a short-term problem.

3.7 Delegation and MBO
Delegation is not an activity distinct and separate from MBO. They are complementary and associated activities, and where a system of MBO is in operation, the negotiating process concerning the objectives of the individual (delegatee) will be concerned with the exact nature of the responsibilities and authorities he is to assume. At the same time the criteria for measuring and assessing performance will be laid down.

3.8 Centralisation and decentralisation
These terms concern the degree to which authority and the power to make decisions are delegated into the lower levels of the operation.

A centralised organisation is one where authority is retained at a high level within the organisation and where top management wishes to control directly the activities taking place. A centralised approach has the advantage of securing greater uniformity of action and effort.

In contrast, a decentralised approach sees much delegation into the lower levels of the organisation, with the authority to act given to more junior members of staff, which acts as a positive motivation. This approach also has the benefit of not requiring too comprehensive and costly a control system.

In practice neither a wholly centralised nor a wholly decentralised organisation of any size is practicable. In the former case, with no delegation the senior members of management would have to do everything, and in the latter, there would be no means of securing any form of unified activity. Organisations tend to lie towards one extreme or the other, according to the management style they have adopted.

It may be too that, for example, in a chain of hotels, some aspects tend towards a centralised approach whilst others tend to emphasise more local authority. Unit managers would have authority to buy perishable produce locally, perhaps from one or more of a number of nominated suppliers, but supplies of say, wines and spirits, would be at prices negotiated centrally and supplied against indents. A unit manager might have the authority to recruit staff, but might be required to check with a centralised Personnel Department before dismissing a member of his staff, in order that the complexities of employee legislation might be taken into account.

There is no one right way to structure an organisation or to delegate within it. Circumstances vary and whereas the small hotel, managed by the owner may be almost wholly centralised, the degree of decentralisation and delegation in larger concerns varies considerably according to circumstances and management choice.

4 ORGANISATION RELATIONSHIPS

The process of delegating responsibilities to a range of subordinates creates organisational relationships between superiors and subordinates, and also between staff at similar levels in the hierarchy but not necessarily in the same department.

The usual method of representing these relationships is by means of an organisation chart, which helps to define the organisational relationships and also gives a picture of all the component parts to help understanding of the whole. The organisation chart is a model of reality. Organisations consist of people working together, interacting with each other, making contact with people outside the organisation and with those who come to use the services provided by the organisation. This is a living, dynamic process and as such cannot be adequately represented in static form.

Nevertheless, the chart does enable the structure of the organisation to be studied, and it also shows the channels through which authority and accountability flow. A number of different methods of illustrating the ways in which an enterprise can be organised have been developed, three of which are described here.

4.1 Line organisation

A line organisation is one of direct, vertical relationships, which links people at each level with their superior and with their subordinates. Delegation and authority flow vertically downwards from the point at which they originate to point at which action is required. Communication, information, feedback and suggestions flow upward along the same line and through the same stages. A line relationship therefore is that which exists between a subordinate and his superior at any level in the organisation. In a pure line structure, the chief executive has authority over every type of activity in his unit and is accountable for the achievement for the unit's objectives and consequently must control buying, marketing, production, administration, personnel, etc.

This approach has the benefit of identifying the individual who carries complete accountability, and certainly it leads to speedy decision-making, since no conferences with specialists are needed. Moreover, it is easy for staff to understand exactly where they fit into the organisation and who their boss is. The major disadvantage is that few people have the necessary expertise to enable them to control adequately every aspect of all the activities involved.

Where the company is fairly small, the advantages tend to outweigh the disadvantages.

A typical line organisation chart for a small hotel might be shown thus:

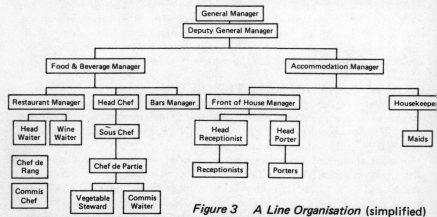

Figure 3   A Line Organisation (simplified)

The 'staff', here illustrated by the Personnel Manager and Personal Assistant are responsible to the General Manager, and advise Line Managers as instanced here by the Food and Beverage Manager and Accommodation Manager, but cannot issue instructions to them by virtue of their own positions.
NB The chart is not intended to show all elements in the organisation

4.2 *Line and staff organisation*

This is an adaptation of the Line structure in which the vertical line relationships are supplemented by a horizontal line of specialist advisors who are usually known as 'staff' and who have no line authority over other executives in the unit. The type of areas in which staff advisors are to be found include Personnel, Marketing and Finance.

There are thus two types of executives in the organisation:

1   Those whose principal task is to achieve the main purpose or objective for which the organisation was formed, eg to provide food and accommodation profitability. These are the Line Personnel.

2   Those whose main purpose is to give help and advice to Line

managers to help them to achieve their objectives. This second group consists of Staff Personnel.

In looking at the authority within each of the groups, it can be seen that each type of executive, Line and Staff, has authority within his own group, ie the Personnel Manager (Staff) has line authority within his own department, just as a Food and Beverage Manager has line authority over those subordinates responsible to him.

In relation to each other, however, it is the job of the Staff group to help, advise and act as consultants for the Line management. The Staff group does not have the authority to direct or impose its wishes on Line management, it is purely advisory.

This approach has the advantage of retaining individual authority in line management coupled with the benefit of specialised advice within the organisation, thus avoiding the drawbacks of one manager having to deal with *all* aspects of the operation and leaving him free to concentrate on his major tasks.

There are potential difficulties in that Line executives are not always willing to seek help from Staff, and it can happen that Staff seek to impose their views and advice on Line management.

Figure 4   A Line and Staff Organisation

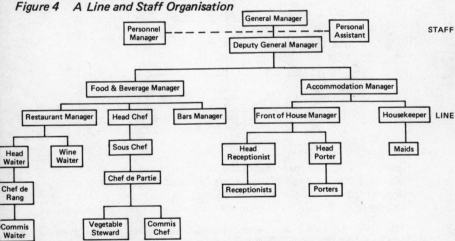

It should be borne in mind, however, that staff executives are appointed by the Chief Executive and resistance from Line managers to suggestions from Staff may well result in instructions to Line managers being issued by the Chief Executive. What is necessary is for Line and Staff to recognise the real need to work together and to co-operate in the formulation of policies, plans and procedures most suitable to the realisation of objectives. The best 'selling' aid to line managers of the assistance and specialist help available from their staff colleagues is the measure of real benefit perceived by line managers from such help in the past. If an accountant, for example, has re-designed a procedure in such a way that reports, records and control information are more easily derived and more quickly available than under the old system, then his advice is more likely to be sought and listened to in the future.

4.3 Functional organisation

A functional organisation is so designed that executives have responsibility for one specific function, delegated to them by the Chief Executive, for example to use the same examples as in 4.2, Personnel, Marketing or Finance. The difference between this approach and the Line Staff approach is that in a functional organisation, the functional executive, who has the requisite specialised knowledge in his particular field of activity has authority over the function he controls in all units within the organisation, and not an advisory role. Thus a unit manager will be responsible to the Chief Executive for his overall results, to the Personnel Manager for matters affecting his staff, and to the Marketing Manager for the marketing activities of his unit, and in respect of these functions will be subject to their instructions.

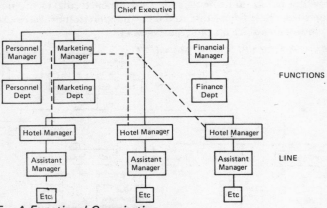

Figure 5   A Functional Organisation
Personnel, Marketing and Finance are illustrative of functional management and the dotted lines indicate that in respect of his own function, each manager can issue instructions to Hotel Managers

However, in a situation where instructions from a functional manager appear to a unit manager to be so inimical to the best interests of his unit, then he would refer the matter to his immediate line superior for advice and resolution.

The advantages come from the benefits of specialisation; on average, a specialist will be better than a non-specialist and will direct and control one function more effectively than someone who has to direct many functions, and it is, of course, easier to train a person to do one job rather than many many. On the other hand, there is a major difficulty in that it does mean that the unit manager is accountable not to a single superior, but to several, each of whom is concerned to see that the duties attached to his particular function are properly executed within each unit.

4.4 Span of control

There has been considerable discussion in management literature over the years as to the number of subordinates a manager is able to control effectively. A conclusion would seem to be that the number should be between three and seven, and that above the higher number, difficulties ensue for the manager.

The argument for a small number of subordinates is that fewer demands are made on the manager's time by his subordinates and in consequence he is better able to concentrate on future planning, which is one of his prime duties. Additionally, of course, he is able to exercise close supervision and precise control, as necessary.

A greater number of subordinates tends to mean that subordinates become more self-reliant and self motivating, develop more rapidly and that there are fewer intervening levels of management.

It is not possible to lay down an optimum number for every situation, because this will be influenced by the objectives of the organisation and by the style of management adopted. Individual units, or groups, will, over a period of time develop the structure which best suits them. This should not preclude a periodic, intense scrutiny of the organisation structure and its efficiency (or lack of efficiency).

5 FORMAL AND INFORMAL RELATIONSHIPS

The emphasis in this chapter so far has been on the formal organisation process and its purposes, but there is a further dimension to be considered. Within the 'official' structure and framework, other informal groupings and relationships develop among groups of individuals with common interests, some of the interests possibly being outside the organisation. Informal groups tend to develop spontaneously and provide a feeling of belonging and security which might otherwise be missing for employees in a large organisation. The basis for informal group formation might be a common interest in a sport, politics, union matters or, as in the majority of cases, a close working association.

Informal groups usually have a leader who acts as a spokesman for the group should that be required and they also develop standards. Such standards might relate to the quantity of work to be done, its quality, or to standards of dress. When norms of this nature are established, those within the group generally conform.

Failure to conform usually meets with the displeasure of the rest of the group and is therefore a potent influence on the individual to do so. Belonging to such groups becomes important to people and anything likely to destroy the status quo is likely to be resisted. This is why there is often resistance to proposed changes in working methods or organisational patterns; people perceive the proposed changes as threats to their existing social patterns.

Management should recognise the existence of such groups and understand the value they have as a means of communication within the organisation which is often speedier and more effective than the formal communications network. Additionally, such groups can be consulted about proposed changes and used as the means of promoting the changes about which they have had a chance to express an opinion. On the other hand, failure to consult and discuss may have the opposite effect. The informal group which does not agree with changes imposed on it is often quite capable (and eager) to frustrate management intentions.

6 ORGANISATIONAL FLEXIBILITY

We live in a changing world, and one moreover, where change is occurring at an increasing rate. Industries have become oriented towards consumers and spend large sums of money on discovering their wants and needs in order that they might be satisfied. The population structure of the country is changing, the birth-rate has declined and there are fewer young people, with the result that demand will fall for all those goods and services consumed by the relative age groups.

In contrast a few years ago ther was a 'bulge' of young people. Each situation presents problems of changing market size and structure which needs to be solved by managers in all industries.

The solution to problems created by change lies in a flexibility of mind and approach. One can ignore change, hope it will not have too much effect on the organisation and probably find oneself overtaken by competitors. Alternatively, change can be seen as a challenge to be met, and an opportunity to be seized.

Social and technological changes are as evident in the hotel trade as in any other industry. The demand for fast food, micro-waves, the micro-chip, computer booking, bargain-break weekends, beds without breakfast are all recent phenomena which have required a new approach rather than a traditional one.

The implementation of change requires sound managerial skills and a continuing supply of information relative to the organisation's operations and to the environment in which it is operating. As changes and trends are detected which require a different response from the unit, so must the situation be analysed and the response planned. This will involve consultation amongst the management and staff concerned the communication of proposed changes to those who will be affected. Careful control must be exercised during the transitional phase and staff motivated until the point where the change has been successfully and completely implemented.

A problem of highly structured, departmentalised organisations is their rigidity and inflexibility. Happenings outside one's own department tend to be seen as 'not my business'. This can be viewed in another way. Since organisations are collections of people, such a view really reflects a closed mind, and part of management's continuing task is to recognise a need for an open mind and a need for re-education and re-training for itself and also for all members of staff.

The ability to recognise the need for change and a willingness to adopt different methods and approaches is not the province of management alone, but a state of mind to be encouraged throughout the organisation.

6
Co-ordination
and communication

1 THE NATURE OF CO-ORDINATION

In dealing with objective setting, MBO, planning and organising, we have seen that as plans are made the jobs assigned to individuals, the work to be done is broken down into smaller and smaller units. The Food and Beverage Manager is in charge of the restaurants, bars and kitchens in his department, and responsibility is delegated by him to waiters, bar and kitchen staff, via heads of departments all of whom have their own parts to play in the achievement of the plans and objectives of the unit at sectional, departmental and corporate levels.

This fragmentation of the work to be accomplished is, of course, the only practical way of getting it done, and it has the advantage of using those with appropriate skills for the specialised tasks involved in running a hotel in a dynamic, changing world. The delegation process, however, by its very nature, does create problems for management to overcome. These problems are associated with the need to make sure that the separate activities take place at the right time, in the right places, in the correct sequence and are completed at the appointed time. As an example, we could consider a banquet or formal dinner. The various courses need to be ready at the right times in the correct sequence, and the component parts of each course must also be ready as required. The appropriate wines must be served with each course at the correct temperature and plates cleared as necessary. These events do not happen correctly by accident, they require a well-trained staff who understand what they are doing, and why. More importantly, they need someone to maintain an effective oversight of all the jobs involved – the manager, who in managing the event is, in fact, co-ordinating the work of his subordinates. Co-ordination is the process whereby work which has been sub-divided is brought together and re-unified in completion of a specific task or objective.

The need to co-ordinate and synchronize the work of individuals is one of the most important managerial activities. Failure to achieve proper co-ordination on a continuing basis will lead to dissatisfied clients, loss of trade and profit with inevitable consequences. It is therefore necessary for managers, especially those at senior level to be able to take an overview of the total operating situation of the unit, and to recognise that the various activities taking place are interdependent. To use the previous example again, the provision of meals requires an adequate lead time for preparation and processing, adequate stocks of food and sufficient staff.

57

preparation and processing, adequate stocks of food and sufficient staff.

Co-ordination is not a periodic activity of management, it must be ongoing. It is also an activity which should pervade an organisation at all levels. A greater degree of co-ordination and, thereby, of efficiency will be achieved where those in the organisation are able to see not only what it is they are to achieve, but how their individual achievement contributes to the objectives of the organisation as a whole. This implies that those concerned do know both what they have to do and also the nature of the overall objective. The imparting of such knowledge requires that they be told. Communication is therefore involved.

2 THE NATURE OF COMMUNICATION

A number of models of varying complexity have been developed to describe communication. In essence the process requires a sender, a receiver, a message, and a means of transmitting the message. Since communication is a two way process, some feedback (at least in an organisational context) is required.

The sender and receiver may be at any level in the organisation, instructions tending to originate in the higher levels whereas information, requests and reports usually come from the lower levels.

The message may be verbal, written, either in words, or figures, or in the form of drawings or may take the form of gestures and facial expressions.

The transmission channel may be the air carrying sound waves, the telephone, closed-circuit television, a computer terminal, or postal systems (internal and external).

Feedback may be immediate in the case of conversation or delayed in the case of written matter, and is essential to show whether the message has been received and understood. A willingness to read or to listen on the part of the receiver is fundamental to the process; without it, true communication cannot take place. Feedback from lower to higher levels is essential to enable management to exercise its control function properly.

3 CO-ORDINATION AND COMMUNICATION

Communication may be defined as a means of giving information in an attempt to influence someone's activities, or as a means of obtaining a response from them either in the form of an activity or another communication as a reply. Without communication it is not possible to achieve effective co-ordination, as, without communication, no one would know what activities require to be co-ordinated.

The order taken by the waiter and passed into the kitchen is a communication designed to achieve a co-ordinated response from kitchen staff and waiters. Reports of stock levels are a communication device enabling goods to be purchased at the appropriate time in suitable quantities. Duty rosters pinned on the staff notice board are the means whereby the right members of staff are present in reception, kitchens bars, etc, at the correct time.

It will be apparent that there is a close relationship between the communication process and the organisation structure.

3.1 Communication and the organisation

Communications within the organisation flow along the lines depicted in figures 3,4 and 5, and in this respect are usually described in terms of their direction within the organisation.

3.1.1 *Downward communication*

This follows the line of command from the point of origin down to the point where action is required, through intermediate points, in the form of commands or orders to be carried out, or the assignment of work to individuals. The General Manager might issue an edict that all members of his staff must improve their standards of personal appearance. Initially this will be passed to his Deputy and then on to subordinate managers and staff.

The restaurant manager might decide to re-allocate tables to waiters and then tell them of his decision. In this context downward communication carries authority and is to be obeyed.

Downward communication may also be concerned with passing on of information eg changes in procedures and methods, changes in personnel, legislation, hours, etc.

Difficulties occur in that a communication passing through all levels in an organisation takes time to do so, but if the originator of the message by-passes intervening levels and deals directly with an individual, this may cause ill-feeling in those he has excluded.

3.1.2 *Upward communication*

This describes how information is transmitted from the lower reaches of the company to senior management. Such information may be a response to a request from management or may be a regular report passed upwards as a matter of routine. The reception staff may be required to report to management the numbers and types of rooms booked or vacant at specific times during the day. Longer term forward bookings may be reported at other time intervals. Much control information of this character flows up the organisation on a regular basis. Details of out-of-the-ordinary occurrences will be passed up to a superior as they happen – the sudden emergency, the request from a tour company to provide lunch today for forty people, is fed into the communications network and the manager makes a decision which is relayed to the enquirer through a subordinate. If the decision is to accept the booking, then all the necessary co-ordinating instructions must be issued to stores, kitchen, bar and restaurant staffs.

The upward communications network is also the means by which subordinates are able to make suggestions, give ideas and make comments to their superiors.

3.1.3 *Horizontal communication*

This term indicates communications between employees at the same level in the organisation, ie those of equivalent status, often in different departments. Communication between staff at the same level in organisation is one of the means whereby co-ordination is achieved. It should be noted that many contacts of this type of an informal nature.

3.1.4 *External communication*

In many industries the majority of staff have no contact with customers and suppliers. The hotel trade is different in this respect and many employees at varying levels in the organisation come into contact with the clientele. The impression created by staff is very significant in creating the image of the unit in the minds of customers and management, therefore, needs to be constantly vigilant to make sure that it is a good one. The obvious areas include reception, restaurants and bars, porters, lift staff and, to a lesser extent, chambermaids. Other contacts by staff ordering goods from suppliers or booking theatre seats or excursions for guests contribute to the image and reputation of the hotel. This may seem unimportant but nevertheless, those who have used the hotel's services do talk about the unit and a good reputation is beneficial; a poor one can damage trade.

4 COMMUNICATION IN THE ORGANISATION

In considering the nature of communication and its directional aspects it emerges that it is communication which enables the organisation to function effectively and that it is a means by which management can control and motivate. In organisations large enough to have been departmentalised, information will emanate internally and also from sources external to the department. Such sources may still be part of the organisation itself or may be totally external to it. Information concerning forward bookings will originate from a variety of external sources and will be subsequently distributed to those departments requiring the information to enable proper planning to take place, and also within such departments.

A unit needs an information system as the means by which the activities of all the individual parts of the whole unit can be guided towards its goal and objectives. The system should gather information from internal company sources and from external sources including market research findings, instructions from Head Office, from newspapers and the trade press or from government departments. All such information requires to be evaluated to determine its importance and management must then decide what is relevant to each section, and the appropriate information must then be communicated to those concerned.

Communication is more than just one of the functions of management. It can be viewed as the basic means by which management can make the organisation operate effectively.

The various means of effective communication can now be considered.

4.1 Verbal communication

Much communication takes place in a conversational setting of which there is no written record, or need of one. A manager issuing instructions to his staff and the chef assigning tasks to his staff are cases in point. An order for goods placed over the telephone is obviously verbal, but confirmation may be required (by either party) in writing. Meetings, for whatever purpose they have been called, are conducted through the spoken word although a record of the proceedings is usually kept. Effectiveness of communication requires the use of clear and concise language and the user should bear in mind both the purpose he is seeking to achieve, the level of understanding his listener(s) can bring to bear, together with their willingness to listen, an essential factor if true communication is to take place.

4.2 Induction

Induction concerns arrangements made by a company to make new employees familiar with the way the company operates, conditions of employment, health and safety, and the employees particular working environment. The length of the induction programme will vary according to the nature of the particular job, its level of difficulty and the previous experience of the new member of staff.

As with any communication, there is the possible danger of giving too much information too quickly and care should be taken to limit the quantity of information given initially, to deal with the essentials first and to give other details over a longer period.

Attitudes towards the nature of information given to employees vary, but details concerning holidays, overtime, pensions, promotion prospects, educational, social and medical facilities are usually provided. Additionally, some companies also give details of turnover, profits, market share, company history and objectives.

Induction is normally a verbal process, which enables questions to be asked, and doubts resolved, supplemented by printed material to be retained and read later.

4.3 Job descriptions

As part of the induction procedure, new employees should receive a job description, which is a document describing the purpose of their job, the duties they have to carry out, the person to whom they are responsible, the people for whom they have responsibility and the standards against which their performance will be measured.

The issuing of such a document removes doubts as to the actual content of a job and it is common for people to be required to sign their job description as an indication of their acceptance of its contents. In describing the duties to be performed, the more junior the job the more detailed the description and conversely, the more senior the job the more general the terms in which the job is described. Many jobs are subject to change, and as changes occur, so they should be recorded in the job description and countersigned.

4.4 Meetings and conferences

Meetings and conferences may be small or large and range from two persons upwards. Some meetings are formal, in that they have specific rules of procedure, others are informal and casual.

The reasons for holding such gatherings include:

(i) to give information, to employees and/or customers or the media;

(ii) to obtain information from customers and/or employees;

(iii) to influence people, eg to encourage employees to try new working procedures enthusiastically;

(iv) to attempt to solve a problem facing the company by bringing to bear on the situation the abilities and experience of those concerned.

To illustrate some of these aspects, we can examine

4.4.1 A conference

Calling together a number of people to transmit information has the following advantages:

(i) everybody gets the details at the same time and there is no need for individuals to re-interpret the information to others

(ii) the avoidance of pressure on other communication channels which would otherwise have to be used and

(iii) to provide a means whereby members of an organisation and/or those who have connections with it get to know each other.

Planning is essential and care must be taken with the administration prior to, during and subsequent to the conference. The time, date, place and purpose must be advised in good time for those involved to make their arrangements and preparation. Where necessary, accommodation and food must be arranged and speakers briefed with care so that their contribution is relevant to the purpose of the conference and is of the appropriate length. If thought desirable, a summary of the talk may be circulated in advance as a preparation for a question and answer session and to stimulate two-way communication.

The chairman must know the purpose of the conference, state it clearly and exercise control so that the purpose is achieved within the timetable laid down.

Any action needed as a result of the conference should be taken quickly, and those concerned should be informed. If there is no implementation of ideas and decisions from previous conferences, then subsequent ones will be devalued in the minds of participants.

4.4.2 Formal meetings

Formal meetings, for example meetings of board of directors have three essential requirements:

(i) that proper notice of the meeting be given to those entitled to attend

(ii) that the meeting be properly constituted, with a properly appointed person in the chair and with a quorum present, and

(iii) that the meeting is held in accordance with the rules, regulations and standing orders.

Strict rules of procedure govern the conduct of formal meetings and cover the agenda, the duties of the Chairman, the formal motions, voting and the keeping of minutes. Such matters are not within the scope of this book.

4.4.3 *Informal meetings*

These are a common feature of everyday business life and the means by which progress is made, day to day decisions are taken and co-ordinated activity achieved. They occur between subordinates and superiors and between people of different sections and departments, as part of the normal routine – eg the regular meetings of the Food and Beverage Manager with those responsible to him to discuss operations for the immediate future.

Meetings may also be called to deal with a particular problem – falling restaurant sales, a sudden increase in the number of staff leaving, a sudden spate of over-bookings for example. Those with a possible contribution to make will be invited, and discussion may result in a proposed course of action. Should the problem be solved, the meeting will not be reconvened; if a solution is not found, then further meetings may be necessary.

Meetings designed to improve internal communication may be a feature of organisational operation and fall somewhere between the formal and informal. Downward communication along the lines of authority is easy, upward communication less easy, and horizontal communication, essential to co-ordination, is more difficult still and to achieve this, it is common for management to have meetings designed to keep themselves and their counterparts informed.

Much communication takes place on a purely chance basis through unplanned encounters during the working day and from them the 'grape-vine', the totally informal communication channel comes into operation. Members of informal groups pass on information which is then passed to other informal groups until most members of the organisation have the information, usually in a very short space of time.

4.4.4 *Reports*

A common means of achieving upward communication is the report required of a subordinate by his boss. The form of such reports varies from the monthly departmental control account to the verbal report of some immediate problem. In the latter case, the facts should be presented accurately, coherently and logically to enable prompt decisions and action to be taken.

4.4.5 *Notice boards*

A time honoured way of passing information to staff, and an effective one, especially if the notice board is regularly cleared of out-dated material, and the board is in a prominent position.

4.4.6 *Suggestion schemes*

A good motivator for staff and a useful means of getting ideas for improvements from staff. Although mainly a one-way channel, such schemes can be developed by acknowledging good suggestions, using them and rewarding, in some way, those making them.

4.4.7 *Company publications*

House journals or magazines are an effective means of conveying information to employees, but need to be interesting and regularly circulated. In addition to any periodic publication, many organisations provide employees with a company handbook giving details of policies, rules and regulations, safety procedures, conditions of employment, etc.

4.4.8 *Appraisal interviews*

Previously considered in chapter 3 a properly conducted appraisal interview provide the opportunity for two-way communication between and employee and his superior concerning the way in which the superior feels his subordinate has carried out his responsibilities and also enables the subordinate to comment on the resources and facilities made available to him to help him in his work.

5 PROBLEMS OF COMMUNICATION

5.1 Screening

This is a particular problem with sending reports or passing information to a superior. People often edit out, as far as possible, anything they feel would cause disapproval from their superior and there is a tendency to 'tell the boss what he wants to hear'. For a different reason messages passing down the organisation are subject to modification as they progress, successive managers putting their own interpretation on the message and transmitting or witholding such parts of the message as they choose. In either direction, once it has been screened in this way several times, significant distortion may be apparent.

5.2 Message construction

The clarity of a message depends on the skill of its construction and a clear message will usually be readily understood. A message which is less than clear and precise can, in verbal communication, be clarified through a process of question and answer. A similar written message does not have this advantage and may be completely misunderstood and misinterpreted. The facility for feedback is a significant element in the process and the more prompt the feedback, the less the risks of misunderstandings.

5.3 Reception problems

A major problem to overcome, is to persuade people to listen to or to read attentively and carefully the message being sent. The problems involved here can include trying to evaluate what is being said, as it is being said, ignoring the bits which are difficult or apparently not relevant, becoming angry if the message appears to be critical of oneself, or simply boredom. The development of understanding by the receiver of a message requires an active involvement and a willingness to take part.

5.4 Other problems
Management literature deals in great depth with communication problems and reference can be made by these seeking further information to books previously listed as references.

6 SUMMARY
Communication is the means by which problems are diagnosed and decisions are both made and diffused within the organisation and external to the organisation. It is therefore essential to the organisation which cannot operate without it. The organisation is the result of the formulation of objectives and of the process of delegation of specific responsibilities and the development of individual objectives.

This division of the various activities into departmental and individual elements requires that these various activities are brought together again in a coherent way, ie that they are co-ordinated successfully. This is achieved through communication in its various forms. The method chosen depends on the precise circumstances at the time, but whatever choice is made, it is vital that those concerned should strive for the utmost clarity.

Finally, it should be said that the total body of communication, verbal and written, provides the 'memory' of the organisation, whether contained in peoples memories or in filing cabinets or a computer. The sum of this information is a vital resource of the organisation to be used when necessary to promote the most effective operation.

7
Control

1 THE NATURE OF CONTROL

Planning and policy formulation are well-established as essential management functions. If the plans and the policies which are guides to decision making in the organisation are to be of any real assistance, they must be clearly stated and communicated to all concerned. The next requirement is the adoption of systems to ensure that the objectives and policies are effective and not merely expressions of hope. It is this last requirement which forms the element of management known as 'Control'.

NEWMAN and WARREN[1] describe the primary and secondary aims of controlling as,

'The primary aim of controlling is to ensure that results of operations conform as closely as possible to established goals. A secondary aim is to provide timely information that may prompt the revision of goals'.

The primary aim is the aspect of control which immediately comes to mind when thinking of translating goals, or objectives, into reality. The secondary aim has implications which it is unwise to disregard. Any system of control worthy of the name focusses attention on the differences between actual achievements and planned achievements for the purpose of remedial action being taken as necessary. Remedial action could, in many cases, have elements of disciplinary action or adverse criticism of the manager and staff identified by the control system as having failed in some measure in their work. Before any such action or criticism is applied, senior management must, in fairness, be sure that this is called for by the facts of the case. The revision of goals referred to becomes necessary when external factors differ significantly from the conditions envisaged at the time the objectives were set.

For example, at the planning stage, expected food costs may include an allowance which would be arrived at by taking into account present knowledge of the behaviour of those prices and estimating the most probable movements in the planning period. But, if inflationary effects or freak weather conditions were to force prices up beyond the levels envisaged at the planning stage, then if no revision of goals for the level of food costs had taken place, any attempt at apportioning blame for the consequent adverse variances would be productive of nothing but frustration.

An essential characteristic of a control system is, therefore, a continuous review of information, as it becomes available, to evaluate the continuing validity and fairness of the targets set at the planning stage.

2 THE CONTROL CYCLE

The requirement for continuous review is expressed by the following diagram which illustrates the cyclic nature of control:

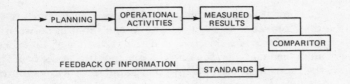

The first box, planning, is open-ended to indicate the receptive attitude towards accepting modifying information which is a pre-requisite for effective planning.

2.1 Standards
In this context, standards are the expression of managerial requirements. They are essential to controlling and must be stated in clear terms, often covering more than one aspect of the results of operational activities. For example, in a given establishment, the number of bedrooms to be cleaned by each chambermaid is one statement describing the standard relating to work output required, but further descriptions concerning the frequency at which constituent parts of the room cleaning job must be done and the quality of cleaning required are also necessary for control.

In general, the quantitative elements of most jobs are relatively easy to measure and compare with standard requirements, but if numerical targets are being achieved at the expense of the quality standards required, then an effective control system must be capable of revealing this.

It is the occurrence of factors which are not so easily quantified which demands careful thought at the stage in the control cycle where results are measured.

2.2 The comparitor
The comparitor is the mechanism by which the measured results are compared with standards to detect any variance from what is required. The variance forms the basis of the feedback of information to management.

What must be emphasised at this point is that the reporting back of information which reveals non-achievement of objectives should be
(i) expressed in a form which high-lights the source of the variance
(ii) prompt enough after the occurrence of the variance not to allow the causative events to continue unchecked
(iii) trigger remedial action by management.

The first of the three points demands a control system which is purposely designed to emphasise the information which it is vital for management to know. In these days of high-speed data production made possible by in-house electronic data processing equipment, it is more than ever necessary to design systems which do not run the risk of burying key information in a welter of data.

The second point is concerned with the frequency with which results should be communicated to management. If the interval between the failure to achieve a given objective and the reporting of that fact to management is too long, then the risk of a continuation of the behaviour leading to the short-fall is run. On the other hand, reports are a source of cost and over-frequent reporting could be excessively costly. A balance must therefore be achieved which tends to minimise the risk of allowing out of control activities to continue and the cost of the control system itself.

The third point may appear too obvious to need stating, but in practice, regrettably, there are numerous instances of full and sophisticated control systems whose warning messages appear to have been ignored by the recipients. Having gone to the trouble and expense of setting standards for achievement and measuring actual results against them, the effort and expense invested will be totally wasted if corrective action, as required, does not take place. In order to avoid this, attention must be given to the design of the system for reporting results, training of all management in interpreting the reports and the development of the management skills required in defining what action is necessary and putting that into effect.

3 BUDGETARY CONTROL

The best known formalised control system designed for the overall statement of objectives and identification of variances from those objectives is Budgetary Control.

ANTHONY and WELSCH[2] define a budget as '... a plan that is expressed in quantitative, usually monetary terms and that covers a specified period of time ...' and list the usefulness of budgets as:

1 for making and co-ordinating plans
2 for communicating these plans to those who are responsible for carrying them out
3 in motivating managers at all levels, and
4 as standards with which actual performances can be compared.

It can be seen that the claims made for budgetary control in the above list agree closely with the control requirements so far discussed as far as the planning, standards setting and comparison of actual results with standards are concerned. A well designed budgetary control system follows the stages given below, usually expressed in periods making up the financial year.

(i) Division of the overall sales, costs and profit objectives into appropriate, departmentalised figures. For example, the total revenue planned would be stated in terms of accommodation sales, bar sales, restaurant sales and any other stated sources of revenue.

Total planned costs would be similarly distributed over the departments incurring them.

(ii) The initial drafts of each department's budget are made available for examination and discussion with the line managers responsible for the attainment of the results. At this stage, the up-to-date, practical experience of the manager concerned can be drawn upon to test the stringency and feasibility of the budget requirements.

(iii) Meetings, as necessary, are held to agree the final budget figures between line managers and their superiors. At such meetings, the relevant information on which the initial figures were arrived at and the reasons which have led departmental managers to dispute the figures may be re-examined and the final figures agreed in the light of that re-examination.

(iv) The complete set of budgets in their agreed form can now be arithmetically reconciled to ensure that they are consistent with the original company-wide plan. Any significant departures from key objectives would necessitate a complete re-think in those areas, which could involve the postponement of certain plans or point to the necessity for taking appropriate action, such as the raising of capital or increasing marketing activity.

(v) The reconciled budgets are now available for the guidance of management at all levels and for receipt of the recorded actual results as they become known.

An apparently simpler, alternative method of applying budgetary control is to have the whole set of budgets compiled by the Senior Managers responsible for the setting of the organisation's objectives and issue each budget as a command. In the description of the system of Management by Objectives in chapter 3 of this book, the importance of gaining the commitment of the individual manager is dealt with. Exactly the same requirement exists in ensuring the effective operating of a budgetary control system. The imposition of performance targets without consultation and participation is unlikely to achieve the third budget usefulness, motivating managers at all levels.

A full description of the mechanics of budgetary control is given in the publication *A Standard System of Hotel Accounting* from the Hotel and Catering Economic Development Council, published by HMSO.

4 OTHER ASPECTS OF CONTROL

It has already been stated that a feature of an effective control system is the speed with which variances from standards are made known so that corrective action may be taken in time to minimise losses. In general, budgetary control systems do not provide such information quickly enough in certain cases. Also, although quality requirements are taken into consideration in budgets of cost, there is usually no overt reference to quality standards in individual budgets. Neither of these points should be taken as shortcomings of budgetary control. Rather, they should be construed as indicators that there are other control mechanisms which are necessary to the management of the organisation. To be able to identify where these other controls on operations are required, it is necessary to analyse the activities involved in the operation and the sources of loss, or any other failures to achieve desired levels of performance which exist, and which, therefore, give rise to the need for a particularised control to be instituted. An example of this approach is given below for the sequence of activities making up the procedures involved from the ordering of foodstuffs through to the sale of the processed material in the form of meals. The sequence shown is intended as an example only of identifiable stages, in fairly broad outline, of the above procedure. Different emphases and titles may be necessary for different sectors of the industry, but the principle of carrying out such an analysis in the context of establishing controls remains the same.

IDENTIFIED STAGE	POSSIBLE SOURCES OF LOSS
Ordering foodstuffs	Use of other than approved suppliers without good reasons. Ordering procedure (eg authorised order form, authorised signature) not followed. Order quantities not consistent with stock control guide lines. Failure to take up negotiated discounts or any other price and terms advantages.
Goods receiving	Deliveries not checked on arrival against the order. No reliable procedure for progressing part deliveries to their completion. Delivered goods not secured in stores immediately after checking. Checking of incoming meats and produce not carried out by a person qualified to assess their quality.
Storage of foodstuffs	Inadequate or poorly maintained records of goods inward and issues. Physical storage requirements to keep foodstuffed in good condition are lacking (eg temperature and humidity controls). Secure area with restricted key holding either lacking or mis-used. No reliable procedure for receiving unused, issued goods back into storage.

	Lack of weighing facilities for the issue of foodstuffs where usage is best controlled by weight.
	Stores' space utilisation poorly planned and hindering the 'first in first out' movements of stocks.
	Too much money tied up in stocks.
Issue of foodstuffs	Issues made without documentary safeguards such as official requisition notes signed by an authorised person.
	Over-requisitioning of goods leading to unauthorised 'sub stores' occurring in kitchen wares.
	Withdrawal of stores unsupervised by any responsible person.
	Lack of forward, short-term planning causing too many calls on stores, thus creating a situation where stores security is likely to become careless.
Preparation, processing and serving	Availability and correct usage of equipment for the most economical preparation of foodstuffs.
	Lack of specifications and checks on the duration of cooking times, weight yields expected.
	No standard recipes, or standard recipes not being followed.
	Lack of portioning equipment or devices to make portion control easier.
	Wastage of food attributable to poor work organisation and/or untrained staff.
	No procedure, or an ineffective procedure for reconciling foodstuffs issued with food sales.
	An unplanned menu which aggravates the problems of forecasting choice and of controlling stores.
	A more than acceptable amount of left-overs frequently occurring, which are not put to profitable use.

To assist in the initial development of control systems for a given establishment, the above approach could be used on all the streams of activities which make up the work of that establishment. In the sources of loss column above, the emphasis is on faults of omission, in the main. The establishment of controls would therefore be the devising of systems designed to provide both essential documentation and desired staff behaviour to remedy those omissions. For example, if it is found necessary to improve the checking in of deliveries, a system of so doing could include a copy order which is to be entered up by the goods receiver and which contains no information on weight or number of packs ordered. Because the checker knows that this copy order will subsequently be checked against the original order, he is more likely to count or weigh delivered items carefully before committing himself to an entry on the form.

Another example, which shows how an identified short-coming may reveal a problem with even wider implications, is where withdrawals from stores may be made by a variety of people and without written authorisation. Further investigation may show that this has become a practice because 'there is no time to fiddle about with bits of paper when stores are required urgently and, after all, the business is about the provision of food, not the production of clerical records'. A response to any argument such as this is that the business is also about the provision of food at a satisfactory profit or within given costs, and that evidence of such lack of control over costly resources tends to suggest that this objective may be in some danger. The key to the problem lies in the reference to shortage of time to carry out desirable procedures. The implication is that insufficient forward planning has been done, generating the necessity for hurried, rushed activities. In the hotel and catering industry, anyone claiming that forward planning will remove the occurrence of all 'panic stations' activity would be guilty of overselling. However, the need to act hurriedly and neglect procedures should be the exception rather than the rule if any measure of control is to be achieved.

5 LABOUR COST CONTROL

The preceding section, describing the identification of control requirements by analyses of possible sources of loss, dealt with the costs of foodstuffs. By far the greatest, single cost in the hotel and catering industry is payroll and payroll related expenses. In a recent study compiled by HORWATH and HORWATH (UK) Ltd[3], the percentages given for the United Kingdom commercial hotel sector were 10.7% for food cost and 34.6% payroll and related expenses. It is therefore clearly important that labour cost is treated as an area for control. Trade publications abound with tables quoting standard figures as guides to what can be expected in terms of work from specified members of staff. The value of these figures is that they may direct attention to departments in a given establishment which vary significantly from these published 'norms', and prompt an investigation into the utilisation of staff which could lead to improvements and cost reduction.

The weakness of such norms is the multiplicity of factors which affect the productivity of the labour force in any given establishment – machinery and equipment provided, quality standards required, size and furnishings of rooms, scope of the menu offered, proportion of convenience foods used and so on. This weakness underlines the need for an examination of what labour costs *should* be in an individual establishment, so that account is taken of all the factors affecting labour cost in a specific situation. This assumes that it is possible to determine a true measure of labour cost for the complex of operations in the various sectors of the industry and is an assumption which will be explored in the chapter on work study.

Any analysis of the possible sources of loss or excessive expense in labour costs must attempt to provide answers to the following questions:
(i) what is the work to be done?
(ii) what effects have changing levels of hotel activity on the amount of work to be done?
(iii) is the necessary work being done in an effective way?
(iv) how much work should be expected from any given member of staff?
(v) how much should be paid for the carrying out of a specified job?

If the answers to these questions are satisfactorily derived by a study of operations in a circumscribed section of the establishment, and if demonstrably improved ways of doing work have been developed, then management has moved towards a position where usable standards for labour costs are available.

Given that justifiable confidence exists with regard to standards for labour cost, control indices which act as yardsticks of labour performance can be developed. These are often arrived at by no more than a simple calculation performed with figures which are already collected for other purposes, so that little extra effort or cost is involved in their calculation. Examples of indices of this type are given below:

(a) Covers per food service staff member:

$$\frac{\text{Number of covers served}}{\text{Number of food service staff on duty}} = \frac{350}{11} = \underline{31.8 \text{ covers}}$$

(b) Food sales per food service staff member

$$\frac{\text{Total sales in restaurant}}{\text{Number of food service staff on duty}} = \frac{\pounds1980}{11} = \underline{\pounds180 \text{ of sales}}$$

This index could also be calculated as the percentage of labour cost to sales for the same situation.

$$\frac{\text{Food service labour cost per shift}}{\text{Total Sales in Restaurant}} \times 100 = \frac{\pounds108.30}{\pounds1980} \times 100 = \underline{5.47\%}$$

(c) Accommodation department staff costs to rooms revenue

$$\frac{\text{Accommodation department staff costs}}{\text{Sales (weekly)}} \times 100 = \frac{\pounds1,142}{\pounds10,040} \times 100 = \underline{11.2\%}$$

Embodying ratios of the above kind into a regular control system can be done by designing a report form which contains the information needed to calculate the ratio and showing the ratio as a column entry on the form. For example, a control sheet for restaurant sales could appear:

			£				$\dfrac{Wages \times 100}{Sales}$
Date	*£* *Sales*	*No of* *covers*	*Average* *per cover*	*No of* *Staff*	*£* *Wages*	*Covers* *per staff*	
21.5.82	1980	350	5.65	11	108.30	31.8	5.47
22.5.82	2460	424	5.80	14	142.90	30.3	5.80
24.5.82	1840	348	5.28	11	108.30	31.6	5.88

EDGE HOTEL MAIN RESTAURANT: DINNER

The example shows the entries for Friday, Saturday and Monday dinners. Extra staff are used for Saturday and the control figures show no significant changes over the three days.

It is emphasised that indices of this kind are of value only if the necessary investigatory work has been done which provides management with a clear idea of what each index should be in order to achieve objectives. If this has been done, then an index is a useful figure as an indicator of whether activities are going according to plan or if remedial action is needed.

6 THE FREQUENCY OF REPORTING

The collection, reporting and evaluation of control data takes time and therefore costs money. Any establishment must ensure that the costs of control systems do not outweigh the benefits derived from them. This is much more easily said than done, because some benefits are difficult to quantify and because the size of an establishment has a most important role in the determination of the nature and frequency of control activity.

A single-unit establishment, where the manager has selected and trained key staff in his own values and methods of operation and where daily close contact is made possible by the small size of the operation, would be unlikely to require extensive control systems. This does not mean that control is less necessary than in a larger organisation, but simply that the scale of the operation and the reinforcement of objectives from frequent, boss-subordinate contact makes possible a less formal approach to control.

The multi-unit, or large single unit, is often organised so that several levels of management intervene between the senior management and the people whose activities directly influence the degree of achievement of the objectives of the organisation. Opportunities for cumulatively serious misunderstandings increase with the number of people who interpret and pass on the original statements of objectives and policy, so that it becomes necessary with larger organisations to devise records and reports which give senior management as clear a picture as possible of the actual results of operating departments compared with expected or budgeted results.

The frequency with which reporting is done is also a factor in the costs of maintaining a system of controls.

The example of a section of a restaurant control sheet given above shows the information under each heading given daily. Daily frequency may be necessary if a control system of this type has just been introduced and it is required to establish the range of movement of each of the variables on the report form. Once these are known the average spend per cover, covers per member of staff and percentage wage costs to sales could be calculated on the weekday and week-end totals only. Note that it is suggested that weekday and week-end results are still kept separate from each other. This illustrates that a control system should differentiate results, so that there is no danger of variances in one set being masked by variances in another. It must be remembered that an important function of control is the focussing of management attention on the precise area to be investigated in the event of remedial action being necessary.

7 DATA PROCESSING AND CONTROL

Until recently, the control on operations, particularly those involving many transactions, has been limited by the amount of time necessary to collect and compare data. Hotels have long had available cash registers with analysis keys which could provide useful information on the sources of revenues. Tying those analysed revenues to costs has been a more intractable problem from the point of view of speed and scarce clerical labour. Micro-computer based systems handling large amounts of data and giving almost instantaneous print-outs of information organised into forms suitable for control purposes are increasingly able to offer management detailed control information only constrained by the ingenuity of the program writers.

An integrated control system developed by a leading company in the electronic data processing field links an advanced cash register to a simultaneous print-out of an order in the kitchen. A micro-processor which could be situated in the manager's office, can also be linked in to provide instant information on the stock position, a sales analysis listing items sold, price, total sales value, percentage of sales value for each menu item and an activity report giving total sales, average value of sales per customer, the labour hours involved, ratios of customers and sales per man hour and percentage of labour cost to sales.

The advent of electronic equipment of this order means that the time-lag between activities and the measurement of their results could be so short that the feedback of information, so essential to control, is available at the touch of a button. This is not to say that management can relax and let electronic circuitry take over, of course. The tasks of planning, the taking of decisions, the functions of marketing and man-management will still need all the managerial skills available, but the ability to evaluate quickly many of the effects of decisions made and, hence, the potential for making increasingly effective decisions, will be much improved.

8 BEHAVIOURAL ASPECTS OF CONTROL

The development and application of control systems have been described in this chapter as important elements of management activity. The mechanics of control have been described as detailed operating budgets and systems developed by analysing sequences of operations to determine where controls are necessary to promote effective working. Some consideration of the effects of control systems on the people whose work is evaluated by those systems is necessary if unproductive conflicts are to be avoided. It is clearly more beneficial to the overall performance of an organisation if managerial actions and procedures are seen by staff as helpful and necessary rather than, say, unduly restrictive and intrusive.

One method of demonstrating to staff the way in which a given control system is both helpful and necessary is to enable them to participate in the system's design. This should reduce the feeling of procedures being imposed upon staff and, by virtue of their being presented with the basic facts of the situation being considered for control, show the necessity for developing a system to achieve control.

There are many instances of control systems developed by specialists such as work study and Organisation and Methods officers, which embody ratios and other measurement devices which seem of great interest to the specialists themselves but which will be unappreciated by line managers and staff with responsibility for the operational areas over which the system is intended to establish control. In such cases, a common development is the leaving blank of columns in the report until the system becomes so weakened that it is a cost with no attached benefits. To avoid this unwanted development and to ensure that control records are properly maintained because they are seen as useful, the controls should have the following characteristics:

(i)   the provision of timely information expressed in terms which are seen as meaningful to the staff whose work is involved

(ii)   appropriateness to the level of management at which they are directed, ie give information on the results of activities over which the recipient of the report has the ability to affect outcomes

(iii) measurement of achievement by the use of factors which are capable of objective measurement.

There is also the view that the more controls that are developed the more time staff will spend in exercising their ingenuity in finding ways to beat the system. While this undoubtedly may be true to varying extents it is a policy of despair to abandon the idea of exercising any controls because of it. In addition, if such a situation poses a serious problem in an organisation, this is more indicative of problems in the industrial relations field, including pay and conditions, than merely in the applicability or not of control systems. The establishment of controls in that event could not profitably begin until the relationships between staff and management have been improved.

Finally, in this section on human reactions to controls, there is a need to avoid the impression that control systems are for the purpose of providing documentary evidence to enable senior management to chastise and harass junior management and departmental heads. A significant improvement in the acceptance of control systems by all levels of staff may be achieved if control information is made available to the level of management whose results are being evaluated against the required standard. The manager concerned must be trained in both the skill to interpret reported results and the range of remedial activities possible in the event of such action being necessary. For example, if a performance index based upon work measured data is used in a report (see chapter 9 on Work Study), the departmental manager concerned should be thoroughly familiar with the bases of the calculation and the implications of the answer. Some variation in this control figure may be unavoidable because they are caused by variations in departmental activity and not by staff, for example, failing to achieve required standards of work performance. The manager must be able to derive a reliable picture of the activity reported upon by taking the information on activity levels and the performance index together and taking remedial action only if this is indicated as necessary after considering all aspects.

References

[1] NEWMAN, W H, Summer, C E and. WARREN, E K, *The Process of Management*, 3rd Edition, Prentice Hall Inc, Englewood Cliffs, New Jersey.

[2] ANTHONY, R N and WELSCH, G A, *Fundamentals of Management Accounting*, Richard Irwin, Inc, Illinois, 1974

[3] HORWATH and HORWATH (UK) Ltd, Report on the UK Lodging Industry, 1982.

8
Purchasing and materials management

1 PURCHASING AS A MANAGEMENT FUNCTION

Purchasing is here defined as the buying in of goods to enable an organisation to function in accordance with its objectives.

So, in respect of both the costs involved and the attainment of quality objectives, this is an area which must receive continuous attention from management.

In retailing organisations and in many manufacturing concerns purchasing is the assigned responsibility of managers who operate at a senior level and have their own clerical support and organisation – often extensive.

In the hotel and catering industry, particularly in the commercial sector, a frequently met feature of purchasing is the division of buying responsibilities among departmental heads such as chefs, housekeepers, bar managers, restaurant managers and control office supervisors. While this may be necessary because of the departmentalised nature of many of the purchases, it is suggested that special care may be necessary to ensure that this divided responsibility receives supervision from senior management to ensure that:

(i) purchases are made which do support the organisation's objectives
(ii) clerical procedures are designed and used to facilitate control over purchasing
(iii) those members of staff with purchasing responsibilities have received sufficient instruction in good purchasing practice to enable them to carry out their responsibilities effectively.

Also, the importance of good relationships with suppliers is of obvious benefit to any organisation which depends upon the availability of goods of specified quality and reliability from outside sources. It is the way in which the purchasing and subsequently the accounting functions are practised which will determine the type of relationships which will be formed with suppliers. The day-to-day contact between the organisation and its suppliers is not conducted by senior management, but by their agents – order assemblers, despatchers and drivers on the suppliers side and the purchase clerks, good receivers and storekeepers of the receiving organisation. This emphasises the importance of having purchasing policies and procedures which are designed to create mutually satisfactory commerce between supplier and receiver and provide documentary evidence that procedures are being followed.

2 PURCHASING AS A PROCEDURE

The variety within the hotel and catering industry regarding sectors of the industry and unit size within sectors makes for difficulty in discussing the extent of the responsibility of any member of an organisation who carries out purchasing duties. For the purpose of this chapter then, the components of a purchasing procedure are examined and the question of which member of management bears responsibility for which part of the procedure is not treated, as these are decisions which can only be made with reference to a particular organisation.

The aims of the purchasing function are:

(i)   to buy goods which give the best value for money and which are consistent with the quality standard and company image required
(ii) to ensure that the organisation actually receives the goods ordered and to be paid for
(iii) to ensure that goods purchased are put to the use for which they were bought
(iv) to make payment for the goods received in accordance with the terms and conditions of trading agreed with the supplier.

Thus, the purchasing procedure could be summarised by noting that it covers the ordering, receiving, storing, issuing and paying for goods received.

2.1 Ordering of goods

Ideally, the ordering of goods should be governed by use of an official order form signed by an authorised member of management. The order should be made sufficiently in advance of the need for the goods so that any difficulties such as non-availability, price change or altered pack sizes can be satisfactorily settled without causing disruption to the work of the organisation.

Having said that, it must be recognised that the hotel and catering industry experiences situations where unexpectedly high demand, or the organising of functions at unusually short notice cause the ordering procedure to be set aside. Telephoned orders and even using the organisation's own transport to collect goods required in a hurry will then occur. If there is an observed tendency for this to occur frequently then it indicates the need for an overhaul of whatever method of forecasting demand is in use. Where any short-circuiting of the ordering procedure arises there must be a routine for making sure that as quickly as possible after the non-standard order has been made, the correct document and authorising procedure must be followed and used as proof of order and confirmation to the supplier.

It is not uncommon to find, particularly in small to medium-sized hotels, that difficulties which are experienced in passing suppliers' invoices for payment are mainly caused by ordering procedures having gone by the board in times of crisis. Thus, a reasonable aim for an ordering procedure to have is control over payments to suppliers. This aim will be assisted by documentary evidence from the ordering system to actual receipt of goods being paid for.

Other control aspects of an ordering system depend for their complexity upon the size of the organisation concerned. Small units may well find a simple set of duplicate books, one for each department which buys supplies, affords them all the control needed, provided they are clearly entered and each transaction is dated. The larger establishment will need order forms in sets, sequentially numbered for security and with copies distributed to departmental manager, control office and goods receiving section. The procedure could then include instructions to goods receivers that no goods are to be accepted in the absence of an order and to the manager with responsibility for purchasing, that the order must be checked for price and clear statement of any special terms or discounts which have been negotiated with the supplier.

On receipt of the goods, the receiver would check the physical delivery against the order, make any alterations necessary and pass the retained copy of the supplier's delivery note with the copy order to the control office to be used for checking the invoice before payment of it.

One remaining question is the amount of goods to be ordered at one particular time. A discussion on this point is given later in this chapter in section 3 of Stock Control.

2.2 Goods receiving

Once the actual goods arrive, control over them changes from a paperwork procedure to a physical activity. The goods must be thoroughly checked against the order before acceptance documents are signed. If the volume and value of items such as meats, fish and poultry are high, then accurate weighing equipment may be a necessity at the goods receiving point. Any slackness in goods-inward checking is observable by the suppliers' drivers, and while they are no more dishonest than any other section of the population, the temptation to profit by such slackness may well be irresistible.

Having checked the goods, the next stage is to move them into secure stores, registering their receipt on the bin-card, cardex system, computer memory or whatever system is in use for stock recording. In one institutional catering situation, pallets of food stores were frequently left in the goods receiving bay after checking and instances were noted of members of the kitchen staff taking items directly from the pallets for use in the kitchen. It is fairly easy to see why, in this establisment, stock checks were seldom able to reconcile shelf stocks with stock records.

2.3 Storing and issuing of goods

The two aspects of storing which are of concern to management are firstly, the provision of storage spaces which are physically suitable for the stocks as regards space, ventilation, temperature, humidity, cleanliness and, secondly, security.

Fields of study such as food production and food science deal fully with the first aspect and some indication of possible losses because of poor security have been mentioned in chapter 7 of this book on Control.

A brief summary of security aspects is given as follows:

(i) a responsible member of staff named as in charge of stores and stores security and trained in an agreed receiving and issuing procedure.

(ii) an official requisition system to be followed whenever goods are required from store

(iii) secured areas with restricted key-holding (this may need to be supported by fixed opening times for issues which, in turn, will require sound forward planning if it is to work smoothly).

(iv) a stock recording system which is maintained promptly with entries for stock on order, received, issued and in hand

(v) spots checks or perpetual inventory to ensure physical count figures agree with stock records

(vi) receiving back into stores items which are issued but unused.

The perpetual inventory referred to at point (v) above is generally carried out by listing all major value stock items and checking them to a regular routine. The remainder of the stock can be sample checked and, if the sampling is carried out scientifically, the percentage error in the total stock can be found within close limits.

2.4 Payment for goods

Suppliers' invoices should be checked for quantity, price and description of goods before payment is made. This does not imply that there is likely to be a conscious attempt to defraud by the supplier, but simply that genuine mistakes can arise and that part deliveries will require noting and including in the receiving establishments' system for progressing the delivery of the rest of the order.

Many years ago, Marks and Spencer Ltd saved themselves a lot of money by dismantling their procedures for checking invoices because it was costing more to maintain them than the money recovered by the discovery of invoicing errors. This could be a factor to take into consideration when designing a system of invoice checking, but it is as well to remember that Marks and Spencer Ltd is a large and powerful organisation whose suppliers are likely to be on their best behaviour in dealings with that organisation. Other, lesser organisations may not enjoy the same respectful treatment.

Additionally, if skilled purchasing has managed to obtain favourable terms and price, it makes sense to ensure that the fruits of those efforts are reaped by checking the invoice to ensure that the total cost takes into account the negotiated conditions.

3 STOCK CONTROL

The term 'stock control' is used to describe a system of ordering in which the prompting of an order is effected by the amount of stock of an item held in the stores.

The reason why stocks of goods are required at all is so that processing, or any other work dependent upon those goods, can continue uninterrupted by lack of materials. What stock control attempts to do is minimise the total costs related to stocking goods and materials of all kinds.

The costs related to stocks arise from:

(i) ordering costs (clerical labour involved in preparing an order, stationery costs, telephone costs incurred in progressing orders or other queries on orders, and postage costs per order)

(ii) stockholding costs (rent, rates and power and costs of storage space, storekeeper's wages, insurance (if related to stock values carried) and, largest cost of all, the cost of the capital tied up in stock value).

The first group of costs are stated as a sum of money per order and the second set, a percentage figure of the average stock-holding value.

These two components of the total stock costs move in opposite directions. The more items ordered on one purchase order, the less is the ordering cost per item, but as order size increases the average number of items held in stock increases and the stock-holding cost, therefore, becomes higher.

One of the principal aims of stock control is to determine the number of items to order at one time so as to minimise the total of these two costs. This number of items is often known as the Economic Order Quantity (EOQ) and formulae have been developed for its calculation, one of which is:

$$N = \sqrt{\frac{2AP}{R^2C}}$$

where N = the number of items to order at one time

A = demand in £ per year

P = cost per order placed

R = price per unit of stock

C = stock holding cost as a percentage of average stock.

Suppose that the relevant data are as follows:

A = demand per year = £5,000

P = order cost = £3

R = price per unit = £1.50

C = stock holding cost = 15%

$$N = \sqrt{\frac{2 \times 5000 \times 3}{1.50^2 \times 0.15}} = \sqrt{\frac{30,000}{0.3375}} = 298 \text{ units (Economic Order Quantity)}$$

The demand per year in units of stock, on these figures, is $\frac{£5000}{£1.50}$ = 3,333, so that the number of orders to be placed per year is given by $\frac{3,333}{298}$ = 11.18 orders. Because the total cost remains at or near the minimum if between ten and thirteen orders are placed per year, in this case it would be sensible to place an order monthly as a routine, thus ordering this stock item twelve times per year.

To demonstrate the effect of calculating and acting upon an Economic Order Quantity (EOQ), suppose that the organisation concerned had been in the habit of ordering supplies of this item quarterly, ie four orders per year. The cost of doing so is:

		EOQ Costs
Order costs per year = 4 × £3	£12.00	£36.00

Units ordered (approx) = 3,333 ÷ 4 = 833.25

Average stock value = $\dfrac{833.25 \times £1.50}{2}$ = £624.94

Stock holding cost per annum = £624.94 × 0.15 =	93.74	33.53
Total Costs =	£105.74	£69.53

The saving per year on this one item of stock is approximately £37 per annum.

NOTE the figure of the £33.53 stockholding cost for the EOQ situation has been arrived at by halving the 298 units which is the EOQ, multiplying by the unit cost of £1.50 to arrive at the cash value of the average stock (£223.50) and taking 15% of that value.

3.1 Assumption in using the EOQ formula
The application of the formula for determining the Economic Order Quantity as just demonstrated depends on the following assumptions:
(i) that annual demand can be estimated for a period of a year
(ii) that demand is reasonably constant
(iii) that no part deliveries are experienced
(iv) that ordering and stockholding costs are reasonably accurate.

At first sight, these assumptions appear to reduce greatly the applicability of the formula. Assuming that demand can be estimated and that it is fairly constant, for example, might well cause doubts on its applicability to stocks in the hotel and catering industry. There are, however, ways of eliminating the need for these assumptions by modifying the basic formula or by using computation methods based on actual information as it becomes available. A full explanation of these methods is beyond the scope of this book, but a useful presentation is to be found in 'Quantitative Approaches to Management' by LEVIN and KIRKPATRICK.[1]

3.2 Evaluating quantity discounts
Some suppliers offer a discount on goods ordered over a specified amount. In effect, such a discount is a reduction in the cost of the goods concerned. The cost per unit of stock is a component in the calculation of the EOQ, and a reduction in the cost has the effect of increasing the size of the EOQ. To evaluate whether the offered discount is worthwhile, or not, the sources of saving from taking up the offer must be weighed against any increase in costs there may be. It is only if the savings are greater than the cost

increase that the discount should be taken up. The savings result from the lower cost price and (because greater quantities are ordered) reduced ordering costs.

The increase in costs arises from the greater average stock which would be carried and, hence, higher stockholding costs.

As an example of this calculation, if the situation described for the example of calculating an EOQ given above is taken, it was seen that the quantity per order should be 298 units of stock.

If a discount of 3% is offered for orders of 500 units and above, and a discount of 6% for orders of 1,000 units and above, the annual costs of the three alternatives may be examined as follows:

Total annual costs for the three purchasing alternatives

Stockholding cost	298 Units(EOQ)	500 Units(3%)	1000 Units(6%)
Price per unit	£1.50	£1.455	£1.41
£ per order	£447.00	£727.50	£1410.00
Average Stock (£ per order/2)	£223.50	£363.75	£705.00
Annual Stockholding Cost (Average Stock × 0.15)	£33.53	£54.56	£105.75
Ordering Cost			
Orders per year (3,333/no per order)	11.18	6.67	3.33
Annual Ordering Cost = No of orders × £3	£33.54	£20.01	£9.99
Materials cost (3,333 × £ per unit)	£4999.50	£4849.52	£4699.53
Total Cost per Year	£	£	£
Stockholding	33.53	54.56	105.75
Ordering	33.54	20.01	9.99
Materials	4999.50	4849.52	4699.53
	5066.57	4924.09	4815.27

The total cost reduces in both cases, so that accepting the highest discount offered appears advantageous. There are further questions to be looked into before the purchaser commits himself to ordering 1,000 units of this item.

Is the item likely to deteriorate by extending its time in storage? Is the demand level stable enough to be confident that 1,000 units represents approximately 16 weeks' usage only?

Can the greater average stock level be accommodated in the stores without causing any space problems?

If the answers to these questions are all satisfactory, then the 6% discount would be accepted by ordering in batches of 1,000 units.

3.3 The use of the EOQ formula

As in all quantitative techniques, the answers given are dependent upon the validity of data used in the formula. The cost per order is relatively straightforward, although careful thought is required to identify all the costs associated with issuing an order. Stationery and clerical labour are obvious costs and easily computed, but allocating order-associated telephone, delivery and receiving costs may need a more prolonged data collection period before a realistic cost figure is identified.

The stock-holding cost is also made up of several parts, for example stores upkeep, handling costs of stores in storage, deterioration and, perhaps, some part of the insurance costs. But, by far the greatest cost is that of the capital which is tied up in stock. It may be company policy to require, say, at least a return of $12\frac{1}{2}\%$ on any investment made. This could, then, be the base figure for the stock-holding cost to which could be added the other costs mentioned above to arrive at the final figure. It is convention to state the stock-holding cost as a percentage of the average stock value for an item because, clearly, there is a strong relationship between the value of the goods in store and the stockholding costs as outlined.

Even with modern facilities for data processing, the up-dated calculation of EOQ measures for every item of stock would not be done by most managements. An approach which is used to reduce the number of calculations involved is to classify the range of stocks according to the amount of capital tied up in each item and establish, say, three classifications: high-value stocks for which EOQ is used, medium value stocks whose maximum and minimum stock levels are continuously supervised, and low-value stocks which are operated on maximum and minimum value levels without absorbing an unwarranted amount of management time.

A further advantage of the study of stock behaviour and associated costs is that it should emphasise to management that significant costs can be needlessly incurred in this field. The true cost associated with ordering is often underestimated until the procedure for its discovery is carried out and, in many cases, the cost of supporting the capital invested in stocks is unappreciated until investigations of this nature are made.

4 MATERIALS MANAGEMENT

The aims of materials management are to
(i)   ensure that the materials purchased are fit for the use intended
(ii) minimise the materials cost by controlling their use and treatment.

The 'fitness for use' aim depends for its achievement on full specifications both of the use and the materials concerned. A simple example of the development of these specifications is the purchase of new floor covering. Consideration of use would require clarification of where the floor covering is positioned, what density of traffic it will be required to withstand, the type of decor into which it must fit and the length of time estimated before its renewal. A full specification of use is an aid to making a good decision on the actual purchase. In this example, the supplier would be in a position to advise on durability and types of covering to choose from if appraised of the full facts of the situation.

In the case of food purchases, the expertise is normally available within the establishment as to the purchasing options open. However, this is not to say that management can rely upon the best purchasing decisions being made as a matter of course in this area unless, once again, constructive thinking produces specifications to act as guidelines. The training and experience of a particular chef may be such that he considers no ingredients but 'the best', nor does he make use of the many pre- or partly-prepared ingredients available. This may be a case for the chef's manager to investigate and, in company with the chef himself, establish and agree the cost saving specifications which the chef may have ignored. In the course of an investigation of this type, a high quality and expensive frozen meat dish was being bought in and the hotel had both kitchen labour capacity and freezer capacity to spare. The decision to make better use of both underutilised resources by making the dish on the premises reduced costs and provided a product comparable in quality to the bought-in dish.

4.1 Value analysis

The technique of value analysis has been developed to assist in the formulation of specifications which, while meeting in full quality requirements, yet aim at minimising product costs. Many companies form value analysis committees to investigate fully all aspects of production, materials to be used and so on. In hotel and catering situations attentions could be directed to the ingredient lists for major menu items and the skill of the committee members would be exercised in seeking lower cost, substitute foodstuffs, or re-assessing ingredient specifications to achieve the same customer satisfaction at lower cost.

On the housekeeping side, the quality of materials available and their range of prices would be investigated against the background of what is required of the materials purchased. For example, if the policy is to change decor in the public areas of the hotel every five years, then perhaps paying for qualities of carpeting with twice that life expectancy might be reconsidered.

Similarly, all recurrent, significant expenditure on materials could be investigated by committees constituted of people able to contribute to the matter under discussion and clear as to the purpose of the exercise – the reduction of costs coupled with the maintenance of required standards.

As is the case with all techniques of this nature, preliminary identification of areas where its application would be worthwhile is essential. The individual item's unit cost is not always the best indicator of the applicability of value analysis. What must be looked for is the total expenditure on a given item. One unit of glassware or crockery does not bulk large in an establishment's accounts, but a study of total, annual replacement costs may well indicate scope for cost reduction. In this example the value analysis group could identify sources and causes and breakages, the robustness of the glassware and crockery in use and then go on to a survey of what goods are available, 'shopping around' to find a desirable combination of durability, appearance and acceptability. It can also be seen from this example that a well-directed investigation has the potential to yield benefits in operating methods such as the handling and safeguarding methods to be used when dealing with breakable items. This aspect could emerge during the investigation into the incidence and causes of breakages, when clear identification of causes can often go a long way towards establishing cures.

4.2 Control aspects of materials management

In the earlier chapter on Control, reference was made to analysing sequences of activities and seeking for possible sources of loss, or wastage, in order to develop control systems designed to minimise these. This approach is clearly applicable to the management of materials from the stage of making the decision to buy from a particular supplier right through to the usage of the bought materials.

In the case of foodstuffs, the management aim is to ensure that proper care and storage are standard practices so that no avoidable waste takes place before use. During processing, trained staff and the correct, well maintained machinery and equipment should assist in obtaining the yields and numbers of portions from given amounts of food inputs.

There is also a significant amount of capital invested in linen, furnishing fabrics, carpeting and other floor coverings, cleaning materials and equipment, glassware, crockery, cutlery and so on. All these items should be purchased according to good, purchasing practice and their management not left to chance. Stock checking is an obvious way to initiate control, but, as discussed in section 4.1 on Value Analysis, further management action to achieve lower operating costs is highly desirable. Additions to costs are caused not only by pilferage, but careless handling and the lack of correct care and maintenance routines. After the years of formal instruction in accommodation management which have been available to entrants into the hotel and catering industry, there must by this time be many members of the industry's management who have the training to identify shortcomings in this area and, given time and opportunity, the ability to devise systems of materials management which could achieve cost reductions when thoughtfully applied.

The problem in all industries is the harnessing and direction of the know-how to be found among all levels of managers in order to achieve a fully controlled operation. This does not happen spontaneously, but must be consciously engineered, having as the start point the relevant objectives of the organisation and moving via systems and procedures, tailored to the needs of the establishment, towards the goal of full use of all resources.

4.3 Standards setting for the control of wastage
Standards set for food and labour cost control have been described in

chapter 7 and it should be apparent that the standards for the utilisation of foodstuffs come into this field of materials management. It would be useful to be able to establish standards which would assist in the control of the costs of all materials, and the purpose of this section is to illustrate how this may be done.

If bed linen costs are taken as an example, the task is to arrive at a workable guide for management to enable them to recognise whether the actual costs incurred are in line with those expected. The 'expected' costs are the result of the attempt to set a standard for bed linen costs by the approach described below.

(i)   Identify the costs involved – bed-linen purchases, laundering and linen repairs.
(ii) Obtain linen stock figures by physical stock check, noting numbers in use, in linen store, laundering, repair and on order.
(iii) Using room occupancy ratios, seasonally expressed if necessary, and taking into account the frequency of linen changes, calculate usage of bed linen during average weeks.
(iv) Working from current stock figures and basing usage on a proper rotation of bed-linen stocks, calculate laundering costs, assess probable repair costs and assess the number of articles to be scrapped as outworn. (This assumes that the laundering and repair costs of bed-linen are recorded for subsequent comparison with those calculated.)

From this collection of information and calculations it is now possible to assess the expected costs of purchasing, laundering and repairing bed-linen and to use these as a standard against which to compare the actual costs. Note that the calculations are based upon an expert view of the wearing quality of the bed linen and the sound management of stocks. If the standard is a significantly lower figure than actual costs, then an investigation should be undertaken to discover if present practices are responsible for the adverse variance.

An approach on similar lines to the above could be developed for any of the major costs associated with materials usage and replacement. A guide to the selection of areas where investigations of this type are likely to contribute to cost reduction is the analysis of each department's expenses, taking the expenses in descending order of amount spent as the order of priority.

5 VARIETY CONTROL

Wide varieties of goods and services offered for sale bring in their wake increased costs caused by the need to carry extensive stocks. Extensive stocks of goods increase those expenses associated with monitoring stock levels, re-ordering and the physical reception and storage of many different commodities. In addition, a wide range of activities is demanded of staff in support of an output of wide variety. This can reduce productive efficiency by a loss of time in preparing and clearing away before and after short production runs.

In a small number of cases, where an organisation is set up to provide 'anything the customer asks for', wide variety presents no problems because the prices of goods and services are high enough to yield satisfactory profits. In the more typcial commercial organisations and in the non-profit-making sectors of the hotel and catering industry, unnecessary variety has often grown more by accident than by design.

The following notes describe a procedure for identifying and controlling excessive variety.

5.1 Simplification, standardisation and specialisation

Simplification, in the context of variety control, is the process of reducing the number of types and varieties of a product to eliminate unnecessary variety.

Before a product or range of products can be simplified, it is necessary for management and the technical experts in the area concerned to agree upon the standards required for the products with regard to quality, composition, method of processing and method of measuring how the products compare with standards.

An example of this type of standardisation could be the examination of a menu, not necessarily with the aim of reducing the variety offered to customers, but for reducing costs and labour in the preparation of menu items.

This examination would require the presence of the managers responsible for the kitchen and menu design and any others in a position to contribute to the discussion. The intention would be to examine ingredients lists, checking that standard recipes are established using the minimum number of ingredients to achieve the desired results. This may be assisted by considering the use of pre-prepared mixes – one stock item instead of several. Also, although restriction of customer choice is not the start point of these variety control discussions, it is clear that a useful contribution may be gained by the availability of figures reflecting the popularity of the various items on the menu. If the demand for certain menu items has declined, then perhaps their exclusion from the menu could achieve a reduction of unwanted variety causing little or no adverse criticism from customers.

The outcome of this exercise should be reduction of unnecessary stock items achieved by standardizing recipes which are agreed upon as producing the right quality of dishes and a total menu which meets the needs and wants of the customers.

It should be noted that this approach does not prevent the development of new dishes for addition to the menu. The design of a new menu item would be controlled by ensuring that the increase in the number of items stocked is at minimum, and then the reception of the new dish by the customers would be monitored to predict whether its popularity is such that the drawing power of the restaurant is enhanced by its continued inclusion in the menu.

This same approach can be applied to any area where uncontrolled variety is causing excessive costs.

The specialisation appearing in the heading of this section refers, in this context, to a policy decision being taken by management to concentrate activities on producing a restricted range of products or services. The advantages of so doing arise from

(i) reduced costs of administation (fewer stocks, easier ordering, fewer suppliers)

(ii) possible development of greater expertise on fewer activities

(iii) a lesser range of skills required by the staff, so producing easier recruitment and, possibly, lower wage costs

(iv) the opportunity to build a sound reputation as a specialist supplier of the particular goods or services offered.

Examples of specialisation in the hotel and catering industry include restaurants specialising in steak dishes or sea-food, hotel groups which offer a grill menu, hotels which market short-stay accommodation for tourists and concentrate on accommodation rather than the provision of food.

5.2 Pareto analysis

A technique which is useful to identify items or stocks which, respectively, are responsible for the bulk of sales revenue or stock value is the construction of a Pareto curve.

Taking stock items as an example, the curve is constructed as follows:

1 list the stock items in descending order of annual usage
2 cumulatively total the column
3 calculate the percentage each item is of the total
4 plot the items (x axis) against percentages (y axis)

It is now possible to determine the items which represent, say 80% of stocks, those representing the next 15% and those which make up the last 5%. Clearly, this presents a good guide to the concentration of control systems on stocks – the items representing the 80% of stocks to receive the closest attention, the next 15% less elaborate control systems and the last 5% the simplest procedure possible.

Pareto analysis can be carried out in similar fashion for revenue earning items, or items' contributions to profit. Here, the analysis directs attention to the array of products which represents a very small amount of revenue, or profit, disproportionate to their numbers and the labour and administration time absorbed by them. These products are the identified candidates for the simplification process. If demand for any one of them is static or declining, if the profit margin is not exceptionally high and if there is no other pressing reason for keeping it (such as to satisfy an important customer) then consideration should be given to dispensing with it.

6 SOURCES OF SUPPLY

The importance to effective purchasing of a thorough knowledge of both individual suppliers and various sources of supply is clear. The selection of the source of supply depends upon the size of the operation and the type of commodity being sought. The buyer for a large organisation using considerable quantities of vegetables, fruit and meat would probably buy at the appropriate market and would develop good relationships with the traders who best met his particular standards on quality and price. The buyer from these sources must, of course be experienced and knowledgeable about the goods being purchased. Smaller organisations might use wholesalers specialising in these goods, selecting the ones with whom to trade by visiting premises and noting those aspects which indicate the efficiency, hygiene and quality level of the warehouse.

The cash-and-carry warehouses are a further source of supplies. Some of the larger cash-and-carry operations have developed sections especially for caterers and also carry wide selections of non-food items which maybe of interest to the hotelier. The disadvantages of this form of buying are that the buyer must supply his own transport for the goods and the account is settled at the time of buying.

Other warehouses have developed into selling wide ranges of goods, giving an advantage to purchasers of being able to buy from one supplier many of their varied needs.

Whatever source or sources of supply are used, it is the duty of the buyer to be continually vigilant as regards the number of suppliers with live accounts and the price and quality of all goods being bought. Too many suppliers, spreading the purchasing power of the organisation thinly, reduces the influence of the buyer with all suppliers, making it more difficult to develop relationships which advantage the buyer's organisation.

Assuming that being a long-standing customer of a supplier automatically guarantees good service and keen prices could also be an error. The buyer's responsibilities should include regular checking to ensure that service, quality and price are all acceptable.

Reference
[1]LEVIN, R I and KIRKPATRICK, C A, *Quantitative Approaches to Management,* 4th edition, 1978, McGraw Hill Kogakusha.

9
Work study

1 THE ROLE OF WORK STUDY

Work study is the most widely used of all the management techniques. Its beginnings concentrated upon repetitive, manual work and its development into international use was based upon applications in manufacturing industries. In earlier days, the practitioners of work study tended to be experts who produced cut and dried solutions to industrial problems which were then imposed upon the work-force. Perhaps the most telling development in work study has been the realisation by its practitioners that if the active cooperation and participation of all concerned – managers, supervisors and workers – is not secured, then full and lasting benefits are unlikely. Another development of the last thirty years has been the rapid spread of work study into occupations other than manufacturing industries. Retail leaders such as Sainsbury Limited have used work study over many years. A survey of organisations advertising for work study personnel in the journal of the professional body of work study practitioners is a cross-section of every imaginable type of organisation – manufacturing, agriculture, warehousing and distribution, hotels, retailing, local authorities – the list is as long as the number of organisation types in the country.

This widespread and varied use of the techniques of work study appears to indicate:

(a) that the techniques are applicable to human work in all its contexts
(b) that the continuing use of work study provides a profitable pay off for its users and can be of benefit to all concerned.

2 DEFINITION AND AIMS OF WORK STUDY

2.1 The British Standards **Glossary of Terms in Work Study** defines work study as follows:

'Work study is a management service comprising those techniques, particularly method study and work measurement, which are used in the examination of human work in all its contexts and which lead systematically to the investigation of all the factors which affect the efficiency and economy of the situation being reviewed, in order to effect improvement'.

A careful reading of this definition reveals the manner in which work study achieves improvements, namely, a systematic identification of all the relevant factors which contribute to the costs of the present method and a systematic development of ways to reduce those costs while maintaining the required quality standards appropriate to the goods or services concerned. The primary aim of work study is making the optimum use of present resources – workers, materials and machinery. Sometimes, a work study investigation may conclude that the answer to a particular problem lies in a radical change to the system of operation, involving the acquisition of new machinery and equipment, but there is no doubt that the commonest benefits are as stated – the achievement of higher productivity from the resources in present use.

2.2 Method study

A further British Standards definition is of the technique of method study:
> 'Method study is the systematic recording and critical examination of existing and proposed ways of doing work, as a means of developing and applying easier and more effective methods and reducing costs'.

There are numerious techniques available in method study for the purpose of recording an exact description of the present method of working so that the elements of that method are presented in such a way that subsequent, critical examination of those facts is made easier. The techniques range from an easily constructed Flow Process Chart (an example of which is used later in this chapter) to time-lapse photography using a cine camera for subsequent frame-by-frame analysis. Whatever techniques are employed it is essential that the aim of the method study investigation, cost reduction, has been to the forefront before the investigation and its method of operating have been decided.

2.2.1 *Reference period data*

To be able to plan the investigation and to prove, later, the efficacy of the outcome, it is necessary to collect data on costs generated by the present methods of working in order to assess the probable savings and to form a comparison with the lower costs of operating resulting from the adoption of the new methods of working. The original cost data must be drawn from records which cover a period of normal working and the period selected should be agreed by an accountant or member of management as being truly representative of normal working. This is so that any later claims made for the financial benefits arising from the application of new methods will be accepted as realistic by all concerned. The period selected is known as the Reference Period. The data should be as full and accurate as possible and some examples of such data are:

Labour cost of the operation
Labour hours of the operation
Output (meals produced, meals served, rooms cleaned)
Range of materials costs per unit of output
Labour cost per unit of output
Labour hours per unit of output.

This information goes on record to provide the basis for comparison with similar data once the new methods are established and in practice.

2.2.2 *The basic procedure of method study*

The importance of a systematic approach to methods improvement is emphasised in the definitions of both work study and method study. The formal Basic Procedure of Method Study is of prime importance in ensuring that method study is carried out in a systematic way. The six stages of the procedure have been adapted from the scientific approach to problem solving, modified to take account of the strong, human implications involved in applying method study.

STAGE 1: *SELECT AND DEFINE THE AREA TO BE INVESTIGATED*
There are several aspects in selecting an area for investigation. Even in a relatively small organisation there is a great deal of complexity and inter-relationships when viewed as a whole. The problem is to select an area which can be defined as to its start and end points and which will provide a worth-while pay-off in relation to the cost of the investigation. It is helpful to consider the selection under the following three headings:

(a) Economic   – operations or departments with high costs or where the present methods of working cause hold-ups in subsequent operations.

(b) Technical   – indications of benefits from the introduction of labour-saving machinery or equipment; opportunities for the introduction of modern production or service systems which will yield calculable and significant cost benefits when compared with present systems.

(c) Human   – sections and departments suffering from excessive labour turnover or undue friction between supervisors and staff; heavy or unpopular jobs.

This first stage of the basic procedure is a survey of the organisation, the result of which should be a planned approach to the order in which work study will be applied to the sections and departments making up the organisation. Using the headings at (a), (b) and (c) above will help to put into perspective the information collected in terms of priority. For example, if a waitress service operation is suffering from the type of problems indicated under the heading of 'human' considerations, these factors may have to be considered as to appropriate action by taking into further consideration data collected under the 'technical' heading. The optimum course of action might well be the development of a self-service system suited to this particular organisation rather than undertaking an investigation aimed at improving working methods and conditions under the waitress service system.

STAGE 2: *RECORD THE PRESENT METHOD OF WORKING IN DETAIL*
The purpose of all the techniques used in recording the details of the present method of working is to present that method in the clearest possible way so that every detail can be evaluated as to its contribution to effective working. Only one technique – the Flow Process Chart – will be

dealt with in this chapter, and the purpose of illustrating that technique is to demonstrate how the recorded present method is critically examined for the purpose of developing improved methods of working. A list of books is given at the end of this chapter to direct the reader towards fuller treatments of the array of recording techniques available to the work study practitioner.

The British Standards definition of a Flow Process Chart is:

'a process chart setting out the sequence of flow of a product or a procedure by recording all events under review using the appropriate process chart symbols'.

The process chart symbols referred to are those of the American Society of Mechanical Engineers, which were adopted by British Standards and are in general and agreed use by work study practitioners.

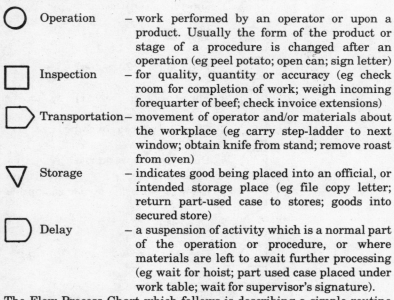

◯	Operation	– work performed by an operator or upon a product. Usually the form of the product or stage of a procedure is changed after an operation (eg peel potato; open can; sign letter)
▢	Inspection	– for quality, quantity or accuracy (eg check room for completion of work; weigh incoming forequarter of beef; check invoice extensions)
⬭	Transportation	– movement of operator and/or materials about the workplace (eg carry step-ladder to next window; obtain knife from stand; remove roast from oven)
▽	Storage	– indicates good being placed into an official, or intended storage place (eg file copy letter; return part-used case to stores; goods into secured store)
⬭	Delay	– a suspension of activity which is a normal part of the operation or procedure, or where materials are left to await further processing (eg wait for hoist; part used case placed under work table; wait for supervisor's signature).

The Flow Process Chart which follows is describing a simple routine which could well be a start-point for a methods investigator at a stage when he or she has been introduced to the department (an institutional kitchen, in this case) and has selected a job which is repeated at least daily and which enables the investigator to get the feel of the department and the department to start getting accustomed to an outsider studying the way that a task is carried out. Because the job is simple, a short time only would elapse between the collection of information and subsequent consultation with all concerned to go some way towards method improvement. This exercise would therefore be a demonstration of the aims and conduct of method study, and, we hope, demonstrate that subsequent studies are not to be feared.

FLOW PROCESS CHART — Operator Present Method Ref No KO 1

Department: *Main Kitchen*   Date: *13.9.82*

Job: *Prepare Sandwich Fillings*   Operator: *Kitchen Assistant*

Job Starts: Instruction from Supervisor

Job Ends: Clean and clear workplace

Instruction from Supervisor

1   Write out requisition note
    (duplicate book, date, goods and quantity)

1   Supervisor's Office

1   Signature

2   Food stores (120 metres)

2   Filling of order (copy kept by storeman)

3   Carry 4 x 6lb cans of corned beef (120 metr

4   Dump cans on worktable

5   Carry can to wall-mounted can opener (7 m

2   Open can

6   Opened can to worktable (7 metres)

Repeat 3 times

6   Empty cans onto table

13 Obtain tray, return to worktable (12 metres

7   Slice meat with knife

8   Arrange slices on tray

14 Tray to next workplace and return (8 metre

9   Clean and clear workplace

	Summary
◯	9
▢	–
⬠	14 (316m)
▽	–
◻	2

96

This chart has headings which identify it as a document in the methods investigation so that if necessary, it can be filed and referred to subsequently. The investigator would, in this case, need only a verbal description from the Supervisor or the kitchen assistant before being able to accompany and observe the kitchen assistant, compiling the chart as the job proceeds. In a more complex piece of work, the observer may have to watch the job one or more times before being able to compile the chart. The distances given on the chart are for the major transportations only and would be estimated by the investigator, not carefully measured.

The chart illustrates a convention often used in this recording technique of showing a loop, or bracket and the number of times a sequence of activities is repeated.

Having recorded the way that the work is carried out, the third stage in the basic procedure is applied.

STAGE 3: *EXAMINE THE DETAILS OF THE PRESENT METHOD CRITICALLY*

Critical examination is often said to be the heart of method improvement. Applied properly, it can also contribute towards gaining the willing acceptance of proposed, new methods of working by both management and workers. The proper application is the encouragement of true participation by all concerned in seeking alternative ways which are easier, simpler and less time-consuming than the present methods and which still achieve the desired end result of the job.

The approach to the development of alternative ways of working is by means of the questioning technique. A form of the questioning technique is —

PURPOSE: What is achieved?
              Why is it done?
                  What else might be done?
                      What else should be done?

PLACE: Where is it done?
              Why is it done there?
                  Where else could it be done?
                      Where else should it be done?

SEQUENCE: When is it done?
              Why is it done then?
                  When else could it be done?
                      When else should it be done?

PERSON: Who does it?
              Why that person?
                  Who else could do it?
                      Who else should do it?

PURPOSE seeks to establish that the activity under scrutiny is necessary to the job, and, if necessity cannot be established, to considering eliminating that activity.

PLACE examines the location where the activity is carried out and searches for the reasons for that location and whether a better location can be found which, for example, could give more space or safety to the worker, or would reduce walking distances and materials transportation.

SEQUENCE is with reference to the order in which an activity occurs in the full sequence of activities making up the job being studied. A change of sequence is being sought which will eliminate or reduce work, or will provide a smoother and more effective work method.

PERSON aims to determine whether re-allocation of the activity to some other person would be beneficial. The other person could be better placed to carry out the activity more effectively. Analysis of a job in this way often reveals that high-skill workers are required to carry out low-skill tasks as part of the job. Could these low-skill parts be re-allocated to lower paid, unskilled workers, thus freeing the high-skill worker for the exercise of his or her skills and reducing the overall labour cost.

MEANS appears as the last of the question sets because it must be established that the activity is essential to the job, that the activity is being carried out in the best place, in the best sequence and by the most effective person before time and capital cost are expended on seeking to introduce the method changes implicit under the heading of MEANS. The changes could range from the provision of purpose designed work aids to assist in locating equipment, or taking the donkey-work from materials handling, to the replacement of manual work by machines. Whatever expenditure is involved in methods changes must be accurately detailed and must be shown to be a worthwhile investment which will provide a return on capital satisfactory to the organisation.

The crucial importance of Critical Examination and close adherence to the Questioning Technique is clearly because this is the stage in the basic procedure of method study where the present method of working is transformed into a demonstrably better method which will increase productivity and reduce costs. It is also the stage where the real participation of all concerned, so essential to the successful introduction of new methods, must be attained. Method study is applied where managers, supervisors and workers have all got strong, vested interests. They are not people unused to the work being studied – indeed, many of them may be well qualified and trained and with pride and interest in the work they do. It is vital that Critical Examination is not misconstrued as an adversely critical attack upon the way that people are carrying out their work. The best way of ensuring that this does not happen is for the work study officer to present the recorded facts of the present method to the people who are responsible for the work and the people who do the work. Ideally, they are the ones who consider these recordings, who define the opportunities for methods improvement and agree the build up of the new method proposals using the format of the questioning technique.

The work study officer would then be a sort of working chairman of such a group with the task of guiding their use of the questioning technique and keeping records of the progress towards the complete, new method. In this way, the new method incorporates the ideas of those responsible for the job and its supervision and stands an incomparably better chance of acceptance than if an attempt to impose new ideas and methods on these people had been attempted.

As an illustration of the working of Critical Examination, the following notes refer to the Flow Process Chart drawn for the preparation of sandwich fillings at Stage 2 of the basic procedure. The technique is shown applied to operation 1 only, for reasons of space.

The first rule is that the operations in order of their occurrence, are the activities first subjected to the questioning technique. The reason for this is that transportations, inspections, storages and delays are centred round operations, so if examination of operations results in their elimination or simplification, the other activities associated with them will be eliminated or simplified automatically.

Operation 1 – 'Write out requisition note'

PURPOSE: Question   What is achieved?
Answer   (i)   A written record showing the goods required.
  (ii)   When signed by supervisor, authorisation for the storeman to issue the goods.

Q   Why is it done?
A   To provide documentary evidence, dated and signed, that the transaction is authorised and to be used in maintaining up to date stock records.

Q   What else could be done?
A   (i)   Telephone request from supervisor to storeman.
  (ii)   Kitchen Assistant goes to stores and asks for goods as instructed by supervisor.
  (iii)   Pre-printed order form with required goods indicated – form to be signed by supervisor.

Q   What else should be done?
A   Pre-printed form, duly authorised.

PLACE: Q   Where is it done?
A   In the Kitchen.
Q   Why is it done there?
A   Because that is the place of work of the Kitchen Assistant who writes out the requisition.
Q   Where else could it be done?
A   In the supervisor's office
Q   Where should it be done?
A   In the supervisor's office (see below for reasoning).

SEQUENCE: Q   When is it done?
A   Immediately before goods are required for processing.

Q Why is it done then?

A Meats, fish and poultry are all drawn from stores in this manner, as part of the accepted practice in the present method.

Q When else could it be done?

A At a suitable time period, depending on forward planning of kitchen activities, before the goods are required.

PERSON: Q Who does it?

A The Kitchen Assistant.

Q Why that person?

A It is the present practice for every kitchen worker who draws goods from store for first processing to write out the requisition.

Q Who else could do it?

A The Supervisor.

Q Who else should do it?

A The Supervisor.

MEANS: Q How is it done?

A Handwritten in duplicate book, giving date, quantity, pack sizes and description of goods.

Q Why is it done that way?

A Accepted practice in the present method.

Q How else might it be done?

A Using a pre-printed form for all stores food items, check off daily requirements in appropriate columns as long before the time they are are needed as is possible.

Q How should it be done?

A Using a pre-printed form and planning ahead as far as possible, so that stores could be assembled and delivered as a batch instead of all the individual trips as now.

Critical Examination would continue by examining in turn the operations 'open can', 'empty cans onto table', 'slice meat with knife', 'arrange slices on tray', 'clean and clear workplace'.

In the course of questioning an activity such as 'slice meat with knife' it is obvious that for speed, better portion control and the elimination of 'arrange slices on tray' as a separate activity, a slicing machine of some type would be considered. This gives a simple example of taking into account other factors before deciding on the capital expenditure of buying a machine – how much would it be used? What are the quantified benefits in terms of labour costs and portioning? What are the costs of cleaning and maintenance of the machine? Only if the purchase cost can be clearly justified would the decisions on whether to buy such a machine and what type of machine – manual or motor driven – to buy.

At this stage of the investigation the form of the recommendations usually begins to emerge. If pre-planning of menus and the use of pre-printed stores sheets is agreed as future standard practice, then the activities carried out by the kitchen assistant of filling in the requisition note, taking it to the supervisor and waiting for the signature, going to the food stores, waiting for the order to be filled, carrying the goods back to the kitchen, are all eliminated from her task with no further work. In their place, the supervisor is required to enter the pre-printed food stock sheets (less writing than previously) and ensure the stores receive the sheet. The stores would then be brought into the Kitchen area by stores staff utilising stores materials handling equipment and making one journey in place of many.

It should now be clear why it is important to subject the operations to critical examination before starting on any other activities. The Flow Process Chart of the original method shows that transportation activities are the most numerous. Attempting to improve methods by starting on the transportation elements of work could have led to either a waste of time in not concentrating initially on the crucial job elements or even have led the examination away from arriving at significant improvements.

Critical examination of the detailed, recorded elements making up the present method is also the reason why a work study investigation improves methods which have been running in their original form unobserved by management and supervision. In a lengthly and complex process it is only by painstakingly analysing the work methods which are employed that the opportunity to see what improvements are possible arises. Such analysis, besides often requiring specialist training takes time and undivided attention – two commodities in short supply among line managers. Thus, no adverse criticism of managers and supervisors is implied in a successful method study investigation.

STAGE 4: *DEVELOP THE IMPROVED METHOD*

At this stage in the basic procedure the task is to draw together into a full and coherent procedure all the selected alternatives generated by the application of critical examination.

Full participation of everyone concerned is still vital to the success of the new method. Indeed at this stage, consultation and the securing of agreement to the changes proposed may be even more extensive than during the work which has gone before. This is especially so if the new method runs contrary to what has been management policy up to now. For example, suppose that the proposed method has significantly reduced the amount of work involved in a group of jobs within a department. At the stage of introducing work study into the organisation, management policy may have included an undertaking that no one would lose his job as a result of the use of work study. Now it can be demonstrated that several staff are excess to requirement in this department. In order to be consistent with stated policy, action must be initiated involving members of management not directly concerned with the investigation until this stage. This might be the suspension of recruitment in other departments and the putting in hand of re-training programmes to fit excess people for jobs elsewhere in the organisation.

Another example is when the proposed method is inconsistent with present policy and the development of the improved method is examined with a view to a possible change of policy. This could happen when the investigation has included the technique of variety control (see chapter 8) and the financial benefits of a simplified menu plan have been arrived at. On the one hand is the current policy on menu planning and on the other the details of the recommended approach, with the financial economies of labour, stock holding and administration fully calculated. Management policy always has priority over the findings of any technique, but, detailed knowledge of what a policy is costing the organisation does not preclude management from changing the policy concerned.

Even in so simple a case as the kitchen operation flow process charted and examined earlier, it can be seen that when this development stage is reached the scope of the investigation widens. As stated, the indications were that all kitchen operations would be pre-planned as far ahead of production as appeared desirable and feasible. The proposals would also involve a change in administration requiring the provision of pre-printed stock sheets. A further proposal made the transportation of foodstuffs, in bulk, to the kitchen a storeman's responsibility instead of using kitchen assistants to bring materials as required. The feasibility of this proposal must be studied and a review of the materials handling equipment carried out.

Finally, agreement must be obtained from stores personnel to this change.

STAGE 5: *INSTALL THE NEW METHOD*
Installation depends upon the following for its success –
(a) Completion of any necessary training of the operators.
(b) Full understanding and agreement by supervisors and operators of the implications of the new method.
(c) Necessary administration details being settled and ready for action – eg control forms, new documentation, wages calculation.
(d) All new equipment, tools and machinery ready, set up and tested.

The more complex and far-reaching the investigation has been, the more need there is for careful planning to make sure that nothing has been over-looked and that the new method can get off to a good start.

This is of particular importance in the hotel and catering industry because the customers are often affected if there is any mistake made. The planning of a complex method installation could be assisted by Critical Path Analysis, which would enable managers with responsibility for the installation to progress events against the network and take remedial action as necessary. The main benefit of using this technique is the establishment of a realistic date for installation. It is beneficial, where possible, to arrange trial runs before there is full commitment to the new method. The importance of a smooth and effective installation is that anything new tends to be regarded with suspicion. A faltering introduction of a new method of working could panic certain managers and cause them to order a reversion to old methods. This need never happen if the installation has been carefully planned and monitored to the stage of application.

STAGE 6: *MAINTAIN THE NEW METHOD AS STANDARD PRACTICE*

The final stage in the basic procedure of method study is intended to ensure that the organisation receives in full the benefits resulting from the new methods of working.

In the period immediately following the installation of new methods, maintenance is carried out by making frequent checks that the new system of operating is being properly followed and taking immediate action if any drift away from procedures is detected.

A longer term view of maintenance is the use of control systems designed to compare the costs and performance of labour after the installation of new methods with the costs and performance data collected for the Reference Period and the calculated standard costs and performances derived from the new methods of operating. The design of the control system will depend upon the data which are selected as being the most important for management to know and to t ke prompt action upon if adverse variances from what is required occur.

Examples of controls of this type will be discussed later when the uses of Standard Times are dealt with.

In practice, many investigations resulting in significant improvements have been marred by failure to carry out adequately this final stage of the basic procedure. This can be caused by the investigator being hurried on to the next investigation before supervising the 'running-in' of the newly installed method, or by insufficient time being spent on designing control documents and training management in their use and significance.

Another fault is in designing extremely complicated control systems with entries which are not fully understood. The tendency in such cases is that both the clerical compilers of the system and the supervisors who should use it become repelled by the complexity and gradually allow the control to degenerate.

2.2.3 *Conclusion of Method Study section*

The importance of following the basic procedure to achieve method improvements cannot be over-emphasised. At first sight it may appear to be a long and tedious process, but there is no doubt that if the procedure is not followed faithfully, the results will fall short of what could be achieved and, in some instances, could cause a disaster because all the implications of proposed changes have not been fully explored.

No mention has yet been made of the part which work measurement techniques can play in method study. Activity sampling and time-study are used in certain recording techniques, and pre-determined motion-time systems are combinations of fine-scale method study and work measurement. This will be discussed more fully when work measurement techniques are described in the next part of this chapter.

3 WORK MEASUREMENT

The British Standards definition of work measurement is:

'. . . the application of techniques designed to establish the time for a qualified worker to carry out a specified job at a defined level of performance'.

Two terms used in this definition are themselves defined by British Standards:

(i) '*A qualified worker* is one who is accepted as having the necessary physical attributes, who possesses the required intelligence and education and has acquired the necessary skill and knowledge to carry out the work in hand to satisfactory standards of safety, quality and quantity'.

(ii) '*Standard performance* is the rate of output which qualified workers will naturally achieve without over-exertion as an average over the working day or shift provided they know and adhere to the specified method and provided they are motivated to apply themselves to their work. This performance is denoted as 100 on the standard rating and performance scales.'

There are four main techniques of work measurement of use in the hotel and catering environment – time-study, activity sampling, analytical estimating and pre-determined motion-time systems. Time-study will be dealt with more fully than the other three because it is the most universally applicable technique in any conditions.

3.1 Time study

The British Standards definition is:

'Time study is a work measurement technique for recording the times and rates of working for the elements of a specified job carried out under specified conditions, and for analysing the data so as to obtain the time necessary for carrying out the job at a defined level of performance.'

To establish the time for the performance of work, as qualified by the above definition, the following conditions must obtain:

(i) The work must have been method studied so that the agreed, new method of working is known to and being used by the person carrying out the work.

(ii) The job must be broken down into its elements of work for the purpose of timing and rating. (See below)

(iii) The person carrying out the time-study must be proficient in the use of the timing device and in the use of the performance rating scale. (See below)

(iv) Care must be taken to include all the time allowances for all the work necessary to the job, particularly those parts of the work which occur only occasionally.

(v) Relaxation Allowance must be computed for the job and applied to the basic Time for the work which is derived by time-study. (See below)

Several terms have been introduced into the above list of points which will now be explained.

The breakdown of the job into elements of work is so that each element can be timed and rated separately. The performance of a worker can vary from one element to another and, additionally, a measured time for each element may be required so that different jobs which have common elements of work can have times synthesised for them without the need for further studywork.

An example of this type of job breakdown is:

The work of a canteen assistant is being time-studied and part of the job is the clearing of canteen tables of used crockery. In the course of this section of the job she wheels a trolley to a position in the canteen, takes a tray from the trolley and walks to the nearest table, where she loads the tray and returns to the trolley to off-load the tray. This is repeated for the other tables in the area, then the trolley is repositioned and further tables dealt with.

A typical list of elements selected for the purpose of the time-study would be as follows:

Element
Number

1	Wheel trolley from kitchen to position in dining area
2	Take tray from trolley and walk to table
3	Load tray with used crockery, cutlery and plastic cups, scraping leavings onto one plate and dessert dish
4	Walk to next table with partially filled tray
5	Carry tray back to trolley
6	Discard plastic cups into container
7	Stack crockery in appropriate positions on trolley
8	Stack cutlery into cutlery container section
9	Move trolley to next position
10	Return with trolley to wash-up.

In this list of nine elements, numbers 1 and 9 are performed as often as a trolley is wheeled empty into the dining area and returned, full, to wash-up. Numbers 2, 3, 4, 5, 6 and 7 are related to the number of times a tray is filled to capacity (not necessarily equal to the number of tables) and number 8 to the number of times the trolley is re-positioned to receive the contents of groups of tables. These frequencies are not likely to be fixed from one cycle of work to another because of the variable nature of what constitutes any particular table's contents. Observations of a sufficient number of cycles of this work must be made to ensure a workable and fair representation of the range of conditions likely to be met with in carrying out this work.

As an example of synthesising times, the wheeling of the trolley is timed and rated separately so that, if need be, a standard time per metre could be synthesised for wheeling a trolley through a work area obstructed by furnishings. Such a standard could then be used in establishing times for similar work without the necessity for further time-studies.

3.1.1 *Rating, or assessment of performance*

Rating is the assessment of the worker's rate of working relative to the observer's concept of the rate corresponding to standard pace. The rating system in widest use in the British Standard scale where 100 corresponds to standard performance which was defined at the beginning of section 3.

The work study practitioner is trained to equate observed performances to numbers on the rating scale, which runs from zero through 100 and upwards to ratings of 150 or 160 which some 'virtuosi' workers could attain. Some verbal descriptions of certain ratings may assist understanding of this method of equating work performances with numbers.

50 rating: Characterised by fumbling, clumsy movements and hesitancy in moving from one element to the next.

75 rating: Steady, unhurried pace of working, often likened to the rate which would be adopted by an unsupervised worker whose payment remains the same regardless of his output.

100 rating: Standard performance – as defined, and described as a brisk, business-like performance.

125 rating: Exhibiting skill well above average with obvious application to the work in hand and using smooth and rhythmic motion patterns.

150 rating: A 'virtuoso' performance, normally attainable only by people who have performed the work very often, are well-accustomed to the tools and equipment and are demonstrating their high skill level.

Rating is arithmetically applied by multiplying the observed time by the selected rating and dividing by standard rating (100). This calculation yields the basic time for each element of work.

The following section of a time study is given to show this in action. It must be noted that the observed times and ratings are recorded during the study and the calculation of the basic times for each element is done after the time-study's completion.

Element No.	Description of Work	Observed Time	Rating	Basic Minutes
2	Take tray from trolley and walk to table	0.08	120	0.096
3	Load tray with used crockery etc	0.64	100	0.640
4	Walk to next table	0.06	100	0.060
3	Load tray	0.75	110	0.825
5	Carry tray back to trolley	0.12	100	0.120

Continued . . .

Continued ...

6	Plastic cups to container	0.09	90	0.081
7	Crockery to trolley	0.74	110	0.814
8	Cutlery to container	0.15	90	0.135
2	Emptied tray to table	0.12	110	0.132
3	Load tray with used crockery etc	0.85	110	0.935
5	Carry tray back to trolley	0.14	110	0.154

This example is based upon the list of elements used as an example of a job breakdown, above. The descriptions of work are not as detailed during a time-study as the full element list, but care must be taken in subsequent documents to describe the work in each element accurately and fully.

It can be seen from this example that ratings above 100 allow a longer time than the worker actually took, at 100 the basic time is the same as the observed time, and below 100 the basic time is less than the time actually taken by the worker. The basic time is thus the time which a qualified worker would take to carry out a specified element of work if that worker is working at standard performance. No allowances for relaxation or interruptions to normal working have yet been included. Inspection of the observed times and ratings also shows that correlation between time taken and performance does not necessarily exist. For example, the first recorded performance of element 3 took 0.64 minutes and was rated at 100, while the second performance of that element took longer but was given a higher rating. This is an important point, because if an observer allowed himself of herself to be influenced by the length of time taken when the actual work content of each performance of a piece of work may be variable – as is the case here – then the time study could be a very dangerous document when the final time allowances based upon it are published. The observer must use rating honestly and must strive to assess each performance of an element of work in accordance with his concept of standard performance, not distorting the rating in a mis-guided attempt to make arithmetic sense.

A closer correlation would be expected if the amount of work is very much the same each time the element is repeated. For example, if laundered bottom sheets are folded in the same way each time, then the elements of unfolding one, spreading it on the cleared mattress and smoothing and folding in edges and corners when carried out on the same size beds would be expected to show a high degree of inverse correlation – as the recorded time becomes shorter, the rating becomes higher.

Time studies of a job of work would be taken until a representative selection of conditions have been covered and enough observations of each element have been recorded to give confidence in the final answer. There are various methods of measuring the degree of confidence which space prevents dealing with here, but which can be studied in the books on work study given at the end of this chapter.

The individual studies have their total basic times for each element of work and the number of occurrences recorded for each element carried forward to a Time-Study Analysis Sheet. This document is used to collect all the information so that, at the end of the programme of studies, the total basic minutes for each element are added to a grand total and divided by the grand total of occurrences of each element. Thus, an average basic time for each element of work is calculated.

3.1.2 *Relaxation and other allowances*
Anyone performing any sort of work continuously will feel the effects of fatigue. If work must be done in a standing position then the worker will need to rest by sitting down at some period. If work is done in a seated position, then relaxation will be taken by the worker moving from the workplace to 'stretch his legs'.

Apart from the posture made necessary by work there is the necessity for refreshment breaks and visits to the lavatory and other factors contributing to fatigue in work which must be considered and allowed for, if applicable to the job being studied, by percentage additions to the basic time for each element of work. These other factors include the amount of muscular strain involved in the work, the ambient conditions in which the work is carried out – noise, temperature and humidity – the degree of concentration and judgement called for and the monotony of short-cycle work. All of these factors contribute to workers fatigue. R M CURRIE's book *Work Study*[2] gives a table for the selection of Relaxation Allowance which is comprehensive and a model which is used by many companies.

In addition to the need to allow extra time for the recovery from fatigue, there is also the necessity to consider interruptions to working which are unavoidable and, therefore, must be allowed for in stating the time to carry out the specified job. In the hotel and catering industry, these allowances, called contingency allowances, are likely to be bigger than in other industries. The reason for this is that work may be carried out in areas frequented by hotel guests who may cause delays by their presence or may require information or directions from a member of the hotel staff who is going about his or her duties. It is clear that whether the job being done has or has not a standard time, the first duty of the member of staff is courteous attention to the guest. It is important that every staff member has been made aware that the time allowed for the completion of work includes allowances designed to cover interruptions of this kind. A further reason is that the flow or sequence of work in an hotel cannot be engineered and organised to the same degree as a manufacturing process, so delays and interruptions can arise from the necessity to consult or be instructed by managers on priorities for various tasks which may change from one day to another. A properly conducted studywork programme will reveal the need for Contingency Allowance and provide the data necessary for arriving at equitable allowances.

The progress towards setting a standard time for a specified job is thus:
(i) Establish the basic time for each element
(ii) Add the selected relaxation allowance percentage appropriate to each element

(iii) Total the resultant standard times at their correct frequency to arrive at the standard time for the job.

(iv) Add any contingency allowance percentage as necessary to arrive at the allowed time for the job.

3.1.3 *Example of the application of time study data:*
Arriving at standard times for room cleaning under specified conditions basic data
Number of Rooms: 106 Singles. 35 Doubles
Expected Average Occupancies:

Monday to Thursday, inclusive.	83% Singles
	10% Doubles
Friday to Sunday, inclusive.	40% Singles
	55% Doubles

TABLE 1   Room cleaning standard times, weekdays, October to March

Description of work	SMs per Occur-ence	Frequency		Frequency per Week	SMs per Week
1 Strip bed, change linen and remake bed:					
Single	4.73	Mon.43+(4 × 88) ⎫	Tue.Wed.	395	1869
Double	6.25	Mon.20+(4 × 4) ⎭	Thu.Fri.	36	225
2 Dust all furniture and ledges and empty waste bins	3.98	All rooms occupied		431	1716
3 Clean bathroom, re-new soap and towel supplies, toilet rolls as necessary	4.63	All rooms occupied		431	1996
4 Renew beverage supplies, wipe clean tray, kettle and supply clean crockery	3.85	All rooms occupied		431	1660
5 Vacuum clean:					
Single	3.82	Single rooms occupied		395	1509
Double	4.96	Double rooms occupied		36	179
6 Final room check	0.60	All rooms occupied		431	259
7 Allowance for maids' trolley usage	0.55	All rooms occupied		431	238
					9651

Season: October to March inclusive.

Bases of frequency calculations:

1 Number of single rooms to be cleaned, weekdays, is 88.
   Number of double rooms to be cleaned, weekdays, is 4.
   Number of single rooms to be cleaned, weekends, is 43.
   Number of double rooms to be cleaned, weekends, is 20.

2 Because of the low average durations of stay, bed linen is changed daily in accordance with management policy.

Allowed time per week =9,651 Standard Minutes
                    or 161 Standard hours

Note The total of standard hours for this work includes a relaxation allowance of 15% and a contingency allowance of 7%.

The column headed, 'Frequency' is the explanation of the average number of times the described work will occur during the part of the week covered by this table. Against 'strip bed, change linen and remake bed', the numbers of single and double rooms to be cleaned on Monday morning (43 and 20, respectively) are given and the numbers of singles and doubles to be cleaned on Tuesday, Wednesday, Thursday and Friday mornings are shown, the expected totals per day being multiplied by four for the four days. The complete assembly of standard time for cleaning duties would require further tables similar in construction to table 1, and covering the week-end room cleaning, the cleaning of corridors and stairways, the cleaning of lounges and all other public rooms and schedules of periodic cleaning, including such operations as the steam-cleaning of carpets, washing down of woodwork and painted surfaces.

The total standard hours collected from each table make up the grand total cleaning standard hours for the period October to March. The same approach would be used for other identified seasonal variations which could be sensibly averaged, so that the number of standard hours for cleaning work over the whole year is established, showing the expected variances season by season. The uses of standard Times will be described later in this chapter.

3.2 Activity sampling

When work is carried out by groups of people, each of whom may carry out different duties during their work, the statistical sampling technique which is the basis of activity sampling may be used. The results of such study will show the percentages of time spent on each of the activities which make up the whole task carried out by the working group.

The Management Services team of a Regional Hospital Board used activity sampling to measure the work of kitchen staffs across the whole range of variously sized hospitals.

Groups of office workers could have their work measured by this technique or, as in the following example, a group of people in the reception area of an hotel.

After consultation with the supervisor and staff involved, to explain the reason for the study and the method of collecting data, the next step is to decide on the list of activities into which the job can be broken down. A study sheet can now be drawn up using the activities as column headings. The method of recording observations is simply to visit to the reception area and make a check mark under the appropriate activity heading, one check mark for each of the members of the reception staff on duty on the shift under observation. The first hundred observations are now used to calculate the total number of observations required for the limits of accuracy selected, to 95% confidence limits.

Assume that the observations taken on the following list of activities are:

Activities	Number of Observations
Deal with guests	19
Telephoning	23
Typing	15
Office work	18
Absent from workplace	11
Present not working	14
	100

'Telephoning' is the activity selected for inclusion in the formula for the total number of observations required and the limit of accuracy selected is 2%.

$$N = \frac{4P(100 - P)}{L^2},$$ Where N = Total number of observations required

P = The percentage of the activity selected

L = Limits of accuracy selected.

$$N = \frac{4 \times 23(100 - 23)}{2^2} = 1771 \text{ Observations}$$

The duration of the study can now be planned so that the number of tours of the workplace necessary to collect the required number of observations can be calculated and the times at which the visits take place randomised.

If it is decided to spread the observations over twenty weekdays to ensure that a representative period of time is covered, then 67 observations per day will be required. Assuming a staff of five (so that five observations per tour are collected), 14 tours per day will give the required number, counting in the initial 100 observations taken. It is vital that the times at which the tours are carried out are at random during the shift, so that any minute of the working day can stand an equal chance of selection. This can be done by using random number tables or by taking cloak-room ticket numbers running from 1 to 450 (7½ hour shift) and drawing for each day 14 tickets at random, letting each number equal the minute of the day when the tour starts. Number 8 would thus be eight minutes after the start of the shift, number 127 two hours and seven minutes into shift, and so on. When the total observations calculated have been taken, the results are summarised as follows:

Activity	Observations	Percent of Total
Deal with guests	390	22
Telephoning	372	21
Typing	319	18
Office work	248	14
Absent from workplace	336	19
Present not working	106	6
	1771	100%

The formula for the calculation of the number of observations can now be written in terms of L (limits of accuracy) to check that the final percentages are within the 2% limit of accuracy selected. The transposed formula need only be applied to the largest percentage; if that is within 2%, then all the lesser percentage will be so.

$$L = \pm 2 \sqrt{\frac{P(100-P)}{N}}$$ Dealing with guests: $L = \pm 2 \sqrt{\frac{22(100-22)}{1771}} + \pm 1.97\%$

which is within the desired limits of accuracy.

It is now known how the time of the five people in reception is spent, given their present duties and given that the average activity of the hotel during the twenty five working days of the study remains the same. The proportions could be applied, if required, to the total working hours to state the hours represented in these percentage.

For example, five staff on this 7½ hour shift is 37½ hours per day. 'Telephoning' is 21% of this time, which is 7.875 hours, or 7 hours 52.5 minutes.

As an indication of the method study aspects of activity sampling, management could re-examine the role of the reception staff in the light of these percentages.

Should tasks unconnected with attention to guests be carried out in the reception area?

Do these tasks interfere significantly with attention to guests? If the amount and type of 'office work' carried out by receptionists connected with the 19% shown against 'absent from workplace'?

The use of activity sampling by the management services team of a Regional Hospital Group, mentioned above, used a form of this technique known as rated activity sampling, which includes performance assessment in addition to the observations taken. This enabled the results to be used to arrive at standard times for the kitchen operations and thus enabled correct staffing of kitchens and the use of a payment system (measured day-work) to improve staff pay and provide detailed control systems for management.

3.3 Pre-determined motion-time systems

These were developed by research which established that all manual work is composed of what are called basic motions. If the conditions under which each of these is carried out are described in a specified way, research showed that a precise time for the motion can be calculated. The 'motion-time' part of the title indicates the main use of these systems – analysis of work to arrive at the best set of motions necessary for carrying out the task, so that the total of the times associated with the resultant motion sequence is minimised.

If just one basic motion – Reach – is taken as an example, the conditions which affect the time to reach to an object will be –

(i)   the distance reached – and

(ii) whether the object is in a location known precisely to the worker or whether the location varies from one cycle to the work of another.

Thus, to make the time taken a minimum consistent with a good, free motion path and to ensure each time that the reach remains the same, attention is focused on good workplace layout and the development of fixtures and holding devices which will assist the worker in achieving and maintaining the best methods of working.

In 1973, Maynard, an American Management Consultant, who had been one of the men responsible for the development of one of these systems (Methods-Time Measurement), was retained by a Regional Hospital Management Board to use the system in setting up methods of working and standard times for catering units.

These systems can be used with success only by experienced work study practitioners who have had a rigorous course of training in their application.

Space prevents a fuller treatment of these forms of combined method study and work measurement, but further readings are given in the book list at the end of this chapter.[3]

3.4 Analytical estimating

In hotel and catering work, analytical estimating is useful to the manager who wishes to assess the time a given job should take to complete, provided that a manager is willing to ensure that he understands the basics of this technique.

The duration of the job is estimated by analysing the work into blocks of work whose time could be estimated more easily than could the time for the whole job.

Example

If the time to lay up restaurant tables is being assessed, the first requirement is a description of the method to be used and a description of any carrying aids such as trays or trolleys. The location of cutlery, cruets, napkins, sideplates and glassware would have to be noted in relation to the disposition of the tables. A sketch of the work area might be the best way to present this information.

The estimator then breaks the job down into elements in their order of occurrence:

1   Collect cutlery, sideplates, napkins etc. and load on trolley
2   Wheel trolley to table 1
3   Position four sideplates
4   Position knives on sideplates
5   Take and fold napkin, position napkin, etc.

It can be seen that once the work of laying four places has been listed the estimator could begin to multiply the time estimates by the number of tables. The other elements of the work such as renewing supplies and walking betweens tables can be easily envisaged and relatively easily estimated as to duration. While this system may not be sufficiently accurate to yield standard times for staffing or payment system design, its uses are –

(i)   to provide a check as to the performance of staff on the work being estimated which might lead to re-training if the indication is that performance may be low

(ii)   the analysis helps the estimator to think through the necessary work involved and may be a good thought starter in providing materials handling assistance and methods of reducing unnecessary movement about the work area.

4   USES OF STANDARD TIMES

4.1   Calculation of the required number of staff

Having established the standard time for specified work it is possible to calculate the number of staff required to perform that work, assuming any level of performance from the staff concerned. Also, because many sectors of the hotel and catering industry experience seasonal peaks os activity, the standard times may be used to calculate staff requirements throughout the year, as the following example shows.

The following occupancy levels are expected in a certain hotel over the forthcoming year.

Period	Weekdays	Weekends
October to March	74%	33%
April and May	80%	49%
June to September	93%	70%

The standard hours for all routine cleaning of rooms and public areas have been segregated into work which is directly related to occupancy and work which is constant regardless of occupancy.

For the period October to March, these standard hours are –

directly related to hotel occupancy   :   324 standard hours, weekdays
(variable)   130 standard hours, weekends
Constant cleaning standard hours   :   125 standard hours per week
(90 standard hours weekdays,
35 standard hours weekend)

What staffing requirements based upon these standard hours and hotel occupancy percentages will be required if cleaning staff work an average 23 hour week and can be expected to achieve an 85 performance on average?

Period	WEEKDAYS Standard Hours		Hours at 85 Perf.	WEEKEND Standard Hours		Hours at 85 Perf.	Number of staff	
	Constant	Variable		Constant	Variable		W'days	W'end
Oct - Mar	90	324	487	35	130	194	21	8
Apr & May	90	350	518	35	193	268	23	12
Jun - Sep	90	407	585	35	276	366	25	16

Notes Hours at an 85 Performance = Standard Hours $\times \dfrac{100}{85}$

Number of staff = Expected work hours (85 performance) ÷ Average working week (23 hours). The method of calculation used gives for each season the total numbers of cleaners needed (29, 35 and 41) indicating separately the number out of each total who would be required for week-end work.

Staff required figures are expressed to the nearest whole number.

4.2 Budgeted Labour Cost
Where budgetary control is applied the labour cost budgets are important parts of forecast, or expected, total cost. Knowing the standard hours of work for the budgeted activities enables a realistic estimate of future labour costs to be compiled.

Where budgetary controls are not part of the control systems it is obviously still advantageous to be able to forecast as reliably as possible likely changes in the number of staff employed and, hence, changes in total labour cost. The standard hours for the work involved at varying levels of activity allow such a forecast to be made.

4.3 Calculation of Labour Performances
The performance of a worker or a group of workers is calculated by

$$\frac{\text{Standard Hours Earned} \times 100}{\text{Attendance Hours}} = \text{Performance Index}$$

Suppose that the standard hours, measured by the standard times of the meals produced in an industrial catering unit, had totalled 243 for a particular week. The attendance hours for that week were 278 in total. The performance of the staff whose work contributed to the standard hours total thus $\dfrac{243 \times 100}{278} = 87$.

If management expected standard performance (100), then this actual performance was sufficiently below standard to have prompted an enquiry into the reasons for this low performance.

The reasons could be a fall-off in customer numbers, or a week of menus unusually low in work content. Neither would be any fault for which the kitchen staff could be blamed.

The reason could also be an undue amount of overtime working which increased the attendance hours, thus lowering the performance index and indicating an unacceptably low level of work performance which calls for further investigation in order to correct it.

4.4 Planning, Scheduling and Allocation of Work

In the example given earlier in this chapter of an application of time study data, the room cleaning duties under specified conditions of hotel occupancy and methods of working showed a figure of 161 standard hours of work. A complete programme of work measurement would provide data which could be treated in a similar way to furnish standard times covering all cleaning duties and duties such as breakfast service, laying-up of restaurant tables in readiness for meal service, the periodic cleaning projects and so on. By the time such a programme is completed, a thorough knowledge of the performance capabilities of the staff involved is available. Coupling this knowledge with the standard times for working enables management to plan work schedules and to allocate work in a fair and consistent way.

'Fairness' works in two ways: the staff are given reasonable work loads and management are not employing people who have not enough work to do.

'Consistency' arises from a comprehensive availability of standard times for all parts of the work and even mixes of work, such as breakfast service preparation and room cleaning. Because work allocation is carried out using those standard hours, whatever work mix is given to a member of staff should present the same requirement for effort and application to work from one day to another.

In these days of centralised kitchens and cook-freeze or cook-chill methods of food production, a knowledge of the standard times for all operations in these kitchens provides methods of scheduling production and ensuring that the production work load is distributed among the staff so that there is both a minimum of ineffective time and equal work loads for all staff.

The central catering section of ICI PLC have standard times available for the production of their varied cafeteria menus which enable the management to work on a standard staffing for each unit and to calculate for each member of the kitchen staff a sequence of duties which is a reasonable workload, so that each individual contributes equally to the kitchen's production. The use of standard times in this case has certainly not produced any lack of variety and appeal in the menus, which compare more than favourably with any commercial cafeteria operation.

4.5 Financial incentive applications

The design of sound, financial incentive systems is a complex field in which it is inadvisable for the amateur to tread, because a badly designed system can do a greate deal of harm. Nevertheless, a sound footing for incentive payments is provided by reliable measures of the work content of the jobs for which incentive payment schemes are being devised.

Excellent schemes have proved themselves over many years in service industries such as cash-and-carry establishments and warehousing operations in food, hardware and pharmaceutical distribution. In all these cases a comprehensive work measurement programme has provided standard times for all operations and the payment system has been a bonus scheme which rewards in relation to a performance index (see section 4.3) and takes into account that a service industry situation is subject to greater day-to-day, or even minute-by-minute, change than the more regulated and planned environments possible in manufacturing industry. There is no doubt that these schemes could be easily adapted for use in the hotel and catering industry, provided that there is equal availability of standard time data.

The variability in hotel and catering operations arises in many ways. For example, an hotel occupancy average figure is taken for a stated period of the year and used to calculate the number of rooms to be cleaned, meals to be prepared and served and so on. Although the average proves to be precise, it is obvious that there will be a variance occurring on a day-to-day basis. Indeed, if this variance is too great it would prevent any worthwhile use of standard times altogether. If this were the case, such a unit should be directing all efforts towards marketing, not work study.

Further variabilities arise because, although a job has one standard time, the actual work content can vary from one performance of it to another. For example, 'Wash, peel and prepare potatoes' is a job title, but variations in actual work can obviously arise when either the potatoes are in excellent condition, with no bruising, regular in shape and with few 'eyes' (lower than average work content) or, perhaps because of frosts and poor delivery, they are in poor condition and need much more preparation work than normal to make them fit for the table. Now, if the work measurement programme has been properly carried out, these variations will have been allowed for to some extent and the staff involved soon realise this. However, if an incentive payment system is employed, then variations which give rise to a greater than average work content can tend to disturb the staff. The disturbance may be passed on to management in the form of complaints and requests for extra allowance of time or money to make up for the extra work.

'Payment by results' systems often heighten the awareness of participating staff to the chances of losing bonus payments.

Thus, against this background of variability, if a financial incentive system is to be used, the relationship between results achieved and financial reward must be carefully designed. This can be achieved by using a selected degree of 'stabilisation' in the basic wage and adjusting the variable bonus part of the wage in accordance with the expected degree of variation in work content. This means that the greater the

variation the less the bonus earnings are as a percentage of the total wage
– ie the less is the incentive to greater effort. If the bonus falls below 15% of
the total wage, then it is questionable whether the incentive system is
worth installing.

This short discussion of financial incentives has dealt with aspects
which are important considerations when considering the use of such
schemes in hotel and catering environments. Space prevents a fuller
discussion of financial incentive systems based upon work-measured data,
but further readings are given in the book-list at the end of this chapter.

5 CONCLUSION

The use of work study in hotel and catering organisations, in both the
profit making and the welfare sectors, is already established. Any
organisation, regardless of size, could benefit from the procedures which
make up work study, and thereby improve the use of its resources. The
basic procedure of method study could be applied by any manager who has
taken the trouble to familiarise himself with the stages in the procedure
and who could be relieved of all other duties for the duration of the method
study investigation. The same is not true of the techniques of work
measurement, when these are being used to establish standard times.
Training in these techniques and supervised practice of them for at least
a year is essential to ensuring that the standard times are valid and can
be safely used for the purposes described in this chapter. In the future, the
increasing development of centralised kitchens and growing use of
cooking procedures where the output of meals can be stored for subsequent
use, will produce growing numbers of applications requiring the
forethought in setting up and the data to achieve minimum cost running
which can be provided by work study.

References and Further Reading

[1] BRITISH STANDARDS *Glossary of Terms in Work Study,* BS 3138, 1959,
London.

[2] CURRIE, R M, *Work Study,* 4th edition, Pitman for the British Institute of
Management, 1977.

[3] MAYNARD, H B, Editor in Chief, Industrial Engineering Handbook,
Section 5, 3rd Edition, McGraw Hill Book Company, 1971.

Introduction to Work Study, Revised edition, 1970, International Labour
Office, Geneva.

SEABOURNE, R G, *Introduction to Work Study and Statistics,* Longman,
1971.

10
Decision making

1 DECISION MAKING AND MANAGEMENT

In examining the various aspects of management in preceding chapters, one element which has been common to all of them is that managers make decisions, either as individuals or as members of groups (formal or otherwise). Frequently the decisions are concerned with the activities of the manager, more often they are concerned with the work of subordinates and what they should do, since it is through 'other people', subordinates, that managers get things done.

Many 'decisions' do not require consideration or evaluation each time they are made. As has been indicated previously, rules and regulations are the result of a previous decision making process where the action to be taken in a particular set of circumstances has been laid down. This type of 'decision' is not the concern of this chapter, which will examine the methodology of dealing with situations which cannot be covered by a set of rules.

The examination of the decision making process falls into two parts, the first being a descriptive approach to the process, and the second being concerned with some simple mathematical models of the process.

Whichever form the process takes, or, indeed, if both are involved, and whether the decision is made by an individual or group, the decision must be made in the light of the goals or objectives towards which the organisation is working, and consequently should be that which is most appropriate to further progress in the direction of those objectives.

2 THE DESCRIPTIVE APPROACH TO DECISION MAKING

2.1 Models of decision making

Many models of decision making have been developed and presented by writers on management and reference may be made to [1]DRUCKER. The factor common to such models is that decision-making is presented as an activity falling into a series of sequential stages, each stage forming the foundation for the next. Also, the models tend to be prescriptive in that they describe the activity as it should be, rather than descriptive in that they illustrate what actually happens. Nonetheless, the provision of such a design for decision making is an excellent means of showing how a logical approach can be used to improve the quality of decisions in an organisation, and various stages of the process are now considered.

2.2 The stages of decision making

2.2.1 *Problem recognition*

A manager is constantly faced with the need to deal with matters involving choice. These may come to his attention through the mail, from sources external to or within the organisation, from staff in the form of a personal approach or from telephone calls, for example. Many will be simple and routine, others will require thought, consultation and information before action can be finally determined.

Information is one of the keys to successful management and much information comes to management in the form of statistical reports, dealing with various aspects of the business and such data will reveal trends in those aspects. In the examples previously used, reference has been made to occupancy levels. Falls in the number of residents or in restaurant occupancy may be gradual and only become obvious as a persistent trend over a period of time, or the change may be sudden and dramatic. In the latter case, it is much more easy to recognise the existence of a difficulty and the need for management action, but both situations have the same potential to damage the organisation if not dealt with adequately.

The art and skill of management lies here in the recognition of the true nature of the problem(s) facing the manager, and of their causes.

Falling restaurant or room sales may result from, for example, one or more of the following causes (amongst others):

prices too high in relation to local competition
poor quality in relation to price
poor quality of food preparation/service
new competition (hotel or restaurant) in the vicinity
a new by-pass or motorway diverting traffic away from the unit
imposition of parking restrictions nearby.

These few examples illustrate the point that a manager must evaluate the whole situation and determine the factors which are creating the problems and how they need to be changed to bring about a resolution of the problem. To do this, he will probably require not only the information he has to hand, but also further data to enable him to analyse the situation as completely as possible.

2.2.2 *Data collection and analysis*

It is not sufficient to know that restaurant sales have fallen from £x per month, week, day, lunch or dinner time to £y. Such knowledge does not permit the problem to be diagnosed or defined. Further information is called for, such as:

– the period over which the decline has taken place
– the rate of decline
– the days/weeks where the decline is most evident
– an analysis of menu items ordered to determine relative popularities
– the number of residents using the restaurant

– the opinions of clients as to the quality of accommodation/meals/ service/prices.

Much information of this nature will be available in the internal records of the organisation, although perhaps not in an immediately usable form, requiring analysis and presentation in a different form to enable it to provide a basis on which to formulate decisions.

Alternatively, it may be necessary to set up some simple information-collecting procedures such as asking restaurant staff to count numbers present at specific times, or to use different coloured order-pads for different days and for lunch and dinner to facilitate data collection and analysis of both numbers of users and also of their orders. Questionnaires can be prepared to enable the opinions of guests to be obtained and recorded. Provided the questionnaire is simple and short, most guests will be prepared to co-operate in its completion, especially if it is explained to them that the purpose is to improve services. Such internal market-research may not be adequate in all cases, and more extensive enquiries may be called for. If the necessary expertise is not available within the company, then external professional assistance from a specialist agency might be required.

It should be recognised that it will usually not be possible to have available all the information which a decision-maker would like. This may be because it is simply not possible to get it, or that the cost of obtaining it might be too high or that the time which would be necessary to obtain it would be so long that it be too late for the purposes for which it is required.

Lack of information is not in itself a reason for postponing a decision; it is better to be aware of the information which is lacking so that due allowance for the missing data can be made.

In the search for relevant information the knowledge and experience of staff should be used. Any individual is the product of his education and experience; the higher a manager rises in an organisational hierarchy the more remote he becomes from day-to-day, detailed operations and consequently the more reliant on information presented to him by his subordinates. Consultation with subordinates and the use of their experience and detailed knowledge of their own particular areas of operation will improve the quality of the decisions made, and may avoid costly mistakes. The willingness to involve subordinates in this way is as dependent on management style as on the quality of subordinates, and management styles range between the dictatorial to the consultative/democratic approach.

The collection and analysis of information and the contribution of staff enable the true nature of the problem to be identified, and once this has been done, the steps to be taken can be considered.

2.2.3 *Alternative courses of action and their evaluation*
The possible courses of action in a particular set of circumstances will usually seem at first glance to be very limited and DRUCKER[2] warns of the

danger of not developing as many alternatives as reasonably possible rather than the two or three immediately apparent choices open to us. The greater the number of choices prepared for consideration, the less likely it is that a wrong choice will be made; there is no guarantee that the correct choice will be made, but the probability is increased.

In our restaurant situation the choice initially could be seen as one of cutting losses and closing or continuing and hoping things improve. Other possibilities might be to:

(a)   close and re-decorate in a different style with a new menu
(b)   change the chef
(c)   re-train the chef
(d)   change the waiting staff
(e)   re-train the waiting staff
(f)   improve food quality
(g)   change prices (up or down)
(h)   advertise to potential local customers (individual or institutional/ commercial)
(i)   reduce the size of the restaurant in an hotel
(j)   increase/reduce the number of covers in relation to price/image changes
(k)   put staff on an incentive scheme for, say, wine sales. Undertake promotional activity, eg a free glass of wine with each meal or two meals for the price of one
(l)   introduce a small band at weekends.

This illustration shows the range of alternatives which can be developed and often this is best produced by a number of people involved with the problem sitting down to determine how to solve it, so maximising the use of staff expertise. In discussion, one person's idea frequently triggers off suggestions from other group members.

Once a range of possibilities has been developed in this way, the advantages and disadvantages of each can be discerned and the range of possibilities narrowed down as those promising the greatest benefits in the circumstances are identified.

Having developed the range of possibilities, some will be eliminated by constraints and restraints both external and internal. The type of licence controls how, to whom and when alcohol is served, health and safety legislation, the availability of money for promotion/advertising, the skill of the chef and other staff all constrain the decision-maker.

When the number of possibilities has been reduced to manageable proportions (say t 5 or 6) the most promising (say 2 or 3) can be evaluated in detail and some of the techniques discussed later can be used (Decision Trees, for example).

From these the final choice will be made, which should, in theory, be that which will enable most progress towards objectives to be made. This is not always possible, and it is sometimes the case that the 'best' decision simply is not possible because of some constraint. If it seems that the answer is to get a new Restaurant Manager, Head Waiter, Wine Waiter and Chef but the cost is beyond the resources of the company, then another alternative must be chosen. SIMON[3] refers to this as 'satisficing' ie not maximising results, but being prepared to accept a level of performance which is satisfactory or adequate. Phrases such as 'a fair share' of the market, 'adequate profit' and 'fair prices' reflect this approach and commonly objectives are set at levels which reflect this approach and look for something less than 100% of occupancy of rooms or in the restaurant.

Choices are made without every possible course of action being considered and evaluated. The cost of so doing in terms of information extraction and the time of the personnel involved would be prohibitive. Moreover, it should also be said that not all managers would make the same choice in the same circumstances and that the same objectives may be realised by different approaches.

2.2.4 *The choice or decision*
The decision will be taken on the basis of the possible outcome of the various possibilities under consideration. The potential benefits and risks will be considered, and the choice will be made on the basis of what appears best in the circumstances to the person charged with making the decision, and his objectives. A decision attempting to maximise profit might well increase the risk element. Conversely a choice minimising risk might well be less profitable.

What is involved is a balancing of the odds, a weighing of the estimated advantages and disadvantages of each possibility in the mind of the decision-maker. An element of uncertainty is ever present. None can predict the future with consistency and accuracy, and the decision can thus never be reduced to certainty however much information or scientific calculation is used in the process.

In the end, the person making the decision is influenced by his experience, knowledge and values and it is according to these that he will make his final choice, and total objectivity is not possible.

2.2.5 *Implementation*
The making of a decision is not a guarantee that it will be carried out. The effectiveness of a decision is contingent on proper implementation. For a decision to be put into effect satisfactorily involves management in consultation, communication and in leadership and motivation.

Decisions involve change; people tend to resist change, and need to be influenced to accept it. Those who are affected should be told in advance of the changes which are to occur. Involvement in the decision-making activity can help by developing an understanding of the current company situation. Prior notification of pending changes in working practices or staffing enables staff to adjust and can avoid the resentment of changes imposed without prior notification.

Those who are required to carry out different duties, at different times or in a different location will co-operate more willingly if they understand the nature of the changes and the reasons for them. Not only those directly affected must be considered but also those on whom the affects will be less direct and obvious. Staff need to know how they will be required to work differently, and also to know how other members of staff will be working in a different way. Communication is therefore required.

The exact method of the communication will, of course, depend on the precise circumstances. In a small unit, meetings with staff on an individual and/or collective basis will probably be most effective. In a large unit or chain then the written word, via notice boards and perhaps letters to employees with personal contact with those most affected may be more appropriate.

The personal, face-to-face approach has much to commend it because it allows for questions and answers. Doubts can be resolved and uncertainties removed and in this way a fuller understanding of the changes resulting from the decisions can be achieved. Proposed changes depend on people for their proper implementation, as does management, and as we have already seen understanding of objectives promotes support for them.

As changes are implemented and progress towards new objectives is made and recorded, so is fresh information generated which enables trends to be discerned on the basis of which further decisions might be made as a result of the controls which have been instituted.

3 QUANTITATIVE TECHNIQUES IN DECISION MAKING

In this section, a brief introduction to some of the techniques used in decision theory is given. Many decisions made by management are arrived at the face of an uncertain future. While no techniques can ever remove the uncertainty of the future, the aim of decision theory is to marshal available information in ways which aim at increasing the rationality of choices made.

3.1 Criteria for decision making under uncertainty

The management of an hotel group have decided to replace traditional waiter serviced lunches with carveries. The investment costs and the increases to revenue expected have been used to arrive at the pay-offs in profit at a given level of sales in each hotel, but there is still disagreement on what level of sales is the safest to calculate upon. The figures of sales provided by market research are re-analysed and grouped under the headings of Optimistic, Most Likely and Pessimistic. These groupings can be named 'states of nature' and referred to as S_1, S_2, and S_3, respectively. If a table is now constructed the various pay-offs under these conditions can be shown against various sizes of investment, ie the number of carveries to be established in the fourteen hotels in the group which are the ones being considered for this venture.

There is a general feeling among the managers that the group should convert as many hotels as they can, consistent with financial safety, to establish themselves in this field before reaction from competition reduces their market.

Pay-off table giving profits over the planning period in £000s

Agreed Decision Alternatives	States of nature		
	S_1	S_2	S_3
Open 4 carveries	115	45	− 2
Open 8 carveries	240	95	− 5
Open 14 carveries	400	170	−20

3.1.1 *The maximax criterion*
Using this criterion leads to assuming the most favourable state of nature (S_1, where sales figures are the highest) and selecting the alternative which maximises the maximum pay-off – in this case, open 14 carveries.

3.1.2 *The maximin criterion*
The assumption here is that sales will conform to the most pessimistic level, S_3, and the selected alternative is the one which represents the best of these three, worst results – in this case, open four carveries.

3.1.3 *The minimax regret criterion*
This criterion requires the calculation of regret values which are arrived at as follows:

Under each state of nature are listed the profits and losses which are associated with the alternatives under this variety of conditions. If the greatest profit, or smallest loss, is taken under each state of nature and the difference between that and all other entries in the column is calculated, then the result is a measure of the 'regret' which would have been experienced if any of the states of nature had occurred and any but the alternative giving the best result had been selected (ie the greatest profit or smallest loss).

The regret table for this example is therefore:

Alternatives	States of nature		
	S_1	S_2	S_3
4 carveries	285	125	0
8 carveries	160	75	3
14 carveries	0	0	18

The maximum regret values under each state of nature are 285, 125 and 18. To minimise regret, the alternative against the minimum of these values is selected – in this case, open 14 carveries.

3.1.4 *The criterion of realism*

So far, three criteria have been shown, two of which provided different answers. The maximax and maximin criteria represent two views as to the likelihood of the best or the worst happening – the former taking an optimistic view of the future and the latter a pessimistic view.

The criterion of realism comes somewhere between these extremes and requires a factor to be arrived at, between 0 and 1, which is a numerical expression of the degree of optimism felt by the decision makers as regards the future state of nature. If the best and the worst are thought to be equally likely, then the factor selected would be 0.5. As the factor moves forwards 1, this is expressing a higher degree of optimism in the most favourable state of nature occuring and, of course, movement towards zero signifies a lessening degree of optimism that a favourable state of nature will occur.

The factor is given the Greek letter alpha $\propto$ and the measure of realism is arrived at by –

$\propto$ (maximum pay-off) $+ - \propto$ (minimum pay-off for each alternative).

If $\propto$ is given the value of 0.6, then application in this case is

4 carveries $(0.6 \times 115) + (0.4 \times -2) = £68,200$ profit
8 carveries $(0.6 \times 240) + (0.4 \times -5) = £142,000$ profit
14 carveries $(0.6 \times 400) + (0.4 \times -20) = £232,000$ profit

The highest profit is against the alternative of opening 14 carveries, so this is the option which would be selected.

3.2 Conditional values and expected values

A conditional value could be described as the result, usually in terms of profit or expense, which will follow given that a certain condition exists. 'If a room occupancy of 85% is achieved, then the net profit on accommodation will be £120,000 for the period', tells us the conditional profit if a stated level of room occupancy is achieved.

In order to calculate what net profit on accommodation could be expected, the likelihood of achieving an 85% occupancy ratio in the period would have to be known. If a probability of 0.7 is calculated, or assessed, then the expected value is arrived at by applying the probability factor to the conditional value –

£120,000 $\times$ 0.7 = £84,000 expected profit.

The following example shows more fully the use of the expected monetary value concept.

An hotel shop has been selling bunches of cut flowers and the shop manageress is reviewing her purchasing with the aim of maximising her profits on flower sales. Overnight, suitable storage facilities for unsold bunches is so limited that she feels that she should work on the premise that what bunches are not sold on the day of their purchase may be regarded as unsaleable. During the current season she pays the wholesaler 30 pence per bunch and retails at 80 pence.

Her first step is to analyse the relevant demand levels for cut flowers and calculate a probability distribution from the analysis.

Sales in number of bunches	Probability
20	0.1
40	0.1
60	0.4
80	0.3
100	0.1
	1.0

Next she tabulates the options of purchasing various numbers of bunches and calculates for each option the conditional value (CV) and the expected value (EV) by using the probability distribution shown above. The option showing the greatest EV is indicated as the buying policy most likely to maximise profits.

		PURCHASING OPTIONS: BUNCHES OF FLOWERS									
		20		40		60		80		100	
Sales	Prob.	CV	EV	CV	EV	CV	EV	CV	EV	CV	EV
20	0.1	10.0	1.0	4.0	0.4	−2.0	−0.2	−8.0	−0.8	−14.0	−1.4
40	0.1	10.0	1.0	20.0	2.0	14.0	1.4	8.0	0.8	2.0	0.2
60	0.4	10.0	4.0	20.0	8.0	30.0	12.0	24.0	9.6	18.0	7.2
80	0.3	10.0	3.0	20.0	6.0	30.0	9.0	40.0	12.6	34.0	10.2
100	0.1	10.0	1.0	20.0	2.0	30.0	3.0	40.0	4.0	50.0	5.0
	Expected Profits	10.0		18.4		25.2		25.6		21.2	

The highest expected profit would be achieved by buying 80 bunches for re-sale. Entries under CV show the result of buying the given number of bunches and the profit or loss if the Sales were as stated. The EV is arrived at by applying the probability of a given number of sales to the CV of each profit or loss.

3.3 Decision trees

A decision tree assists the decision making process by presenting in a graphic form the decision points and the possible outcomes which are elements in the total decision area. The outcomes each have a probability attached to them so that an expected value can be calculated for each route through the tree.

Example

The marketing director of an hotel group with forty-seven hotels distributed throughout England is studying the reports prepared by market researchers and the group's accountants. These reports deal with the launching of a carvery service in the hotels. The service could be launched regionally or nationally, or it could be launched regionally at the beginning to test market demand and then expanded nationally if the demand were favourable.

The reports yield the following information:

A limited introduction in a specified area has a probability of 0.7 of meeting with a large demand and of 0.3 with a low demand. If low demand is experienced the profit yield over the planning period will be £500,000. Large regional demand will indicate the existence of a large national market with a probability of 0.7 and the profit yield would be £2,500,000. However, there is a chance of low national demand, so that the extra costs of expansion would produce a loss of £250,000. If, in the face of this possible loss it is decided not to expand nationally, then the profits would be £1,250,000 under high demand and £1,000,000 if demand is limited.

Turning to a consideration of installing the carveries throughout the group, the marketing manager knew that all the outcomes of the market's reception of the carveries had already been identified as:

(i)   large National demand
(ii) large regional but limited national demand
(iii) generally limited demand.

The profits associated with a national launch were £3,750,000 for large national demand, £500,000 for large regional followed by limited national demand and a loss of £200,000 if demand is limited both regionally and nationally.

The marketing manager presented all the above information in the form of a decision tree. See page 130.

Notes

1   The probabilities for each set of outcomes resulting from a decision must total unity.
2   The two probabilities following 'national launch' are calculated by using the joint probabilities of a large demand regionally followed by a large national demand and a large demand regionally followed by a limited national demand:
    $0.7 \times 0.7 = 0.49$, say 0.5
    $0.7 \times 0.3 = 0.21$, say 0.2

The third probability for generally low demand is, of course, the same whether the launch is regional or national.

The conditional profits at the tips of the branches of the tree can now be multiplied by their respective probabilities, working into the tree so that the resultant expected monetary values can be compared at each decision point. The highest EMV, when all the decision points have had EMVs calculated for them, is an indication of the strategy which will be most profitable.

The calculations can be shown as follows, starting at the tip of the top branch.

£ conditional profits	Probability	£ expected monetary value	
2,500,000	0.7	1,750,000	The highest expected monetary
− 250,000	0.3	− 75,000	value is given by expanding nat-
	1.0	1,675,000	ionally after regional launch which enjoys high demand.
1,250,000	0.7	875,000	Block off the 'stay regional'
1,000,000	0.3	300,000	decision on the tree.
	1.0	1,175,000	
500,000	0.3	150,000	The £1,675,000 is brought back
1,675,000	0.7	1,172,500	from the calculation of EMV for
	1.0	1,322,500	the 'go national' decision. This total will now be compared to the EMV total for a national launch.
3,750,000	0.5	1,875,000	The immediate national launch
500,000	0.2	100,000	of carvery installations shows
− 200,000	0.3	− 60,000	the greatest expected monetary
	1.0	1,915,000	value, so the 'regional launch' decision is blocked off leaving the indicated most profitable strategy – National Launch.

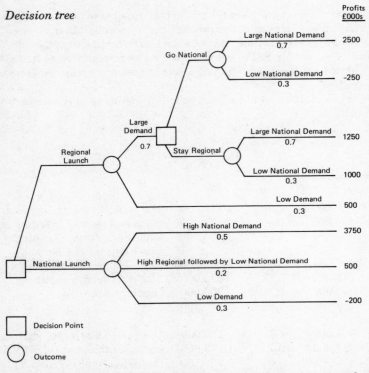

Decisión tree

Profits £000s

Go National
Large National Demand 0.7 — 2500
Low National Demand 0.3 — -250

Regional Launch
Large Demand 0.7

Stay Regional
Large National Demand 0.7 — 1250
Low National Demand 0.3 — 1000

Low Demand 0.3 — 500

National Launch
High National Demand 0.5 — 3750
High Regional followed by Low National Demand 0.2 — 500
Low Demand 0.3 — -200

☐ Decision Point

◯ Outcome

In using any form of expected value calculations it must be remembered that the conditional profits or losses, have not vanished from the scene. In this example a 30% chance of making a loss occurs in two strategies, launching the service regionally and then expanding and going for a national launch immediately. The only strategy which shows no risk of loss is a regional launch with no expansion.

Typically, this is also the alternative which yields lower profits. So management have still a decision to make – play safe for relatively modest profits or go for the indicated best strategy. The ability of the organisation to carry the risk of the indicated losses will obviously play a large part in the final decision.

4 THE VALUE OF DECISION THEORY

The making of decisions which commit an organisation to large investments in the face of an uncertain future is part of the burden carried by senior management. A cursory survey of different industries over the last 20 years is enough to yield examples of entrepreneurs and captains of industry who took decisions which turned out to be disastrous for their organisations. Using hindsight, some of these disasters can be dissected, and business analysts can see that the danger signals were present, but disregarded, long before the final collapse. In other cases, the decision maker appears to have made moves which clearly contributed to the crash, such as expanding in an industry with a limited and well-supplied market and, in another case, behaving as if there would be no reaction from competitors when fierce price-cutting was used as the corner-stone of a strategy.

The value to management of using decision theory is that the techniques are based on collecting information which is relevant to the decision being made and processing that information to obtain the conditions under which a given decision is the best one.

If two managers disagree on the advisability of a certain course of action, it is possible to evaluate which manager is most likely to be right only if their experience, temperaments, willingness to take risks and leanings towards optimism or pessimism are known. Using decision theory, they would be required to support their opinions by a clear statement of the facts which led them to their opposed beliefs and to support their conclusions in debate.

There is always a possibility of even firmly held views and beliefs being modified when all the relevant facts have been presented. A manager may be against a certain plan of action because he is considering only present physical and financial resources. His opinion may be radically altered if, by taking into account the highly probable extra revenues to be earned by following the plan, those resources could be safely increased by raising the necessary finance. The use of the techniques such as payoff tables and decision trees encourages the decision makers to search for all the possible outcomes which might follow the pursuit of a given line of action. Giving these possibilities their due weight before making a final decision must improve the quality of the decisions made.

In the brief outline of some of the techniques which has been given here, probability factors were shown in use. The only indication of how these may be arrived at was in the example of stock decisions to maximise profit on cut flowers.

The arrival at reliable probability values is clearly an important part of decision theory, but restricted space prevents any fuller discussion of the topic here. Yet, it is worth pondering that although a brief presentation of probability may make it appear to be merely guesswork, it is capable of being much more than that. The decisions makers are people of experience and knowledgeable about their own industry and its customers. Guided by either a decision analyst or one of their peer group who has studied decision theory, useful probability distributions may be developed which will clarify the likely outcomes of alternative strategies and improve the chances of the selected strategy being successful.

Reference
[1] DRUCKER *op.cit*
[2] DRUCKER *op.cit*
[3] SIMON, H, *Administrative Behaviour,* 3rd edition, The Free Press, New York, 1976.

11
Network analysis

The aim of this chapter is to present an introduction to the basic ideas of network analysis as applied to relatively modest scale projects. In earlier chapters, the need to plan, control and co-ordinate acivities has been a recurring theme. Network analysis is a technique which was developed to do just that in a dramatic context in America in 1957. The cold war between East and West had given urgency to the need for America to shorten the time to produce inter-continental ballistic missile systems capable of action. The planning and managerial control system which was developed to ensure that the shortest time possible would be taken to complete the ICBM project was given the name Project Evaluation and Review Technique – now known world-wide as PERT. Since then, PERT itself has been used to control massive civil engineering projects and the like, and simplified derivatives of this pioneer networking system, using similar approaches, have been developed and widely used in many and varied organisations. Suitable applications for network analysis are projects where a complex of activities exist requiring the use of different people, as individuals or in groups, in order to carry out those activities and accomplish the objective of the project.

1 STAGES IN NETWORK ANALYSIS

1.1 The identification of all the activities necessary to the completion of the project and the establishment of durations of time for each activity. Network analysis is dependent for its usefulness on the reliability of the time estimates for the activities. If the work involved has been work studied and reliable standard times are available, so much the better. If this is not the case, then estimates of the times must be carefully carried out and checked for reliability as the project proceeds.

1.2 Information collection on the logical sequencing of activities. This stage involves determining how the activities are related, one to another, which activity must be carried out first and how different sequences of activities link together or run quite separately duringthe course of the project. This stage is helpful in preparing to draw the network, but it is common to miss some of these activity dependencies until after the network has been started. A pencil and an eraser are therefore the recommended tools with which to draw and repair the diagram.

1.3 Construction of the network diagram

1.4 Calculation of earliest starts and latest finishes for all activities

1.5 Identification of the critical path

1.6 Calculation of float values for activities not on the critical path

1.7 Presentation of the network in the form of a Gantt chart

1.8 Use the Gantt chart to schedule and allocate work or to shorten the overall project time.

2 CONSTRUCTION OF THE NETWORK DIAGRAM

2.1 There are three symbols used in a network:

(i) a circle, called an event node, which is used at the beginning and end of each activity in the network. If several activities start from or end at one event node, the circle may be elongated to make easier the reading of the network. An event node has no duration and can be thought of as the instant at which one activity finishes and the next starts.

(ii) an arrow, representing an activity. An activity has a duration and uses resources (labour, machinery and capital).

(iii) a broken-line arrow to indicate a dummy activity. A dummy activity is used.

(a) to ensure that each activity has its own, unique pair of start and finish numbers:

(a)

The dummy activity 7,8 is introduced so that activity A and activity B can be identified by 6,8 and 6,7 respectively

(b) to preserve the logic of the network:

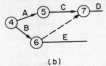

(b)

The dummy 6,7 informs us that the activity B must be completed before activity D can start. Activity D is thus dependent upon activities C and B

Dummy activities have no duration and use no resources.

2.2 When starting to draw the network the activities which could take place at the same time are identified. At this stage, no consideration needs to be given to the number of people available to carry out those activities, nor to the other resources needed for their execution.

Suppose a network is being drawn for the making of a cup of tea. The kettle could be filled, milk and sugar obtained and tea put into the pot all starting at the same instant, so that four activity lines would be shown starting from the same node. If only one person is involved in making the tea, this appears absurd, but it must be emphasised that this principle is crucial to the logic of the network – if an activity is not dependent for its start upon the completion of another activity but it must not be shown in sequence with that other activity but in parallel. Returning to the tea-making, it would be found that a subsequent activity, "boil kettle" is probably of sufficient duration to allow the obtaining of milk and sugar, the tea being put into the pot and any other activities connected with tea-making to take place within it – but this will be more fully discussed later when the uses of the Gantt chart are dealt with.

Activities which are in sequences are next identified and shown to be so, eg, prepare mise-en-place, obtain meat, prepare meat for oven, cook meat. This is an obvious sequence dealing with the human work of preparing a roast for the oven and ending with a machine process of cooking the meat, during which time the cook could be available for other work.

3 CALCULATION OF EARLIEST STARTS AND LATEST FINISHES

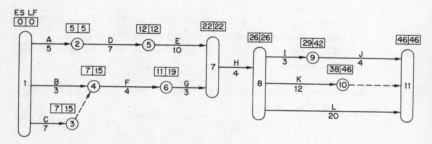

The above network will be used to demonstrate the calculation of earliest starts and latest finishes for the activities in the network. The diagram shows double compartmented boxes at each node. The left hand compartment is for entry of the earliest start time and the right hand box for the latest finish time.

Earliest starts (ES) are first calculated for every activity. The ES for activities A,B and C is put at time zero and, by adding the duration (in days) of each activity, shown below the activity line, the ES for activities D and F are found.

At node 4 there are two possible answers – one being $0+3 = 3$ and the other $0+7+0$(the dummy) $= 7$. Wherever this occurs when calculating ES, the larger, or largest of the numbers is selected as the ES.

Another example of this is the three activities ending at the terminal node, 11. The three answers are 33, 38, and 46. The last number is the largest so it is entered in the ES box of the terminal node.

At this stage the overall duration of the project has been identified as 46 days. This is therefore the latest finish (LF) of all activities, so it is entered in the right hand box over the terminal node and the calculation of the LF for each of the other activities can begin.

The LF are calculated by moving backwards through the network, subtracting each activity duration from the LF figure in the box at its terminal node.

The first three calculations are as follows:

$46 - J(4) = 42$; $46 - \text{dummy}(0) = 46$; at this stage there are three possible answers at node 8, $42 - I(3) = 39$; $46 - K(12) = 34$ and $46 - L(20) = 26$. When calculating LF the smallest of all the possible answers is taken, in this case, 26.

Now note that the LF at the initial node is zero, which it must always be if the arithmetic and method have been done correctly.

4 IDENTIFICATION AND MEANING OF THE CRITICAL PATH

The critical path is the longest time path through the network, so the durations of the activities lying on the critical path sum to the overall project time. These activities are said to be critical in that any delays in their completion will cause the whole project to be late in finishing. In large civil engineering or ship-building contracts there are often penalty clauses written in for over-running the planned completion date, so that identification of those activities which require the closest supervision if the project is to be completed on time is clearly of great benefit to the project managers.

In the hotel and catering industry, refurbishing of sections of an hotel or re-equipping and alterations to kitchens are disturbances to normal operating. Ensuring that the disturbance is kept to a minimum and that a reliable completion date is set is on offer to management by the use of network analysis.

Further, if the overall project time, when calculated, appears to be unacceptably long, the critical path identifies those activities which, if extra resources or efforts are directed to them and their durations shortened thereby, will directly reduce the overall project time.

Once the ES and the LF for all activities are calculated, the activities on the critical path are immediately identifiable. If the diagram in section 3 above is examined, it can be seen that some boxes have the same figures in both compartments. This is the indicator of the critical path. In this diagram the critical activities are A, D, E, H and L.

If the 46 days of the project were thought to be too long a time, then these are the activities which must be shortened if the project time is to be reduced. Activity K is 12 days in duration and could, perhaps, be reduced to half that time by purchasing more modern equipment, say, or by working overtime at increased labour costs. Unfortunately, such increased expenditure would have no effect upon the project's duration and, to that extent, would be wasted, because K is not an activity on the criticial path.

5 CALCULATION OF FLOAT VALUES FOR ACTIVITIES NOT ON THE CRITICAL PATH

Referring again to the network in section 3, boxes can be seen with different figures in the ES and LF sections. At node 4 the ES is 7 and the LF, 15. The difference of 8 days is known as 'event slack' and means that the earliest time at which activity F can start is the end of the seventh day (or morning of the eight), but that its start could be delayed by 8 days and still leave enough time for it and the following activity, G, to be completed before H is scheduled to start at the end of day 22.

Event slack is only a first indication of where there is flexibility in the times for starting activities not on the critical path. In many cases it is necessary to analyse the amount of slack into various types of flexibility in starting times known as 'float values'. Two of the most important types are Total Float and Free Float.

5.1 Total Float (TF)
TF is the amount of time by which the start of an activity can be delayed without affecting the overall project time. This is the difference between the LS and the ES. Calculating total float for activity F is therefore; $LS - ES = 15 - 7 = 8$ days.

5.2 Free Float (FF)
FF is the time an activity's start can be delayed without delaying any succeeding activity if that activity starts at its earliest time.
FF for activity F is : $ES_{(succ)}$ – Earliest finishing time for F

$= 11 - 11 = 0$. So, although activity F has 8 days of total float, because it cannot be started until activity C finishes (7 days) and itself takes 4 days, its earliest finishing time is $7 + 4 = 11$ days, which means that if the succeeding activity, G, starts at its ES time of 11, F has no flexibility to move, ie no free float.

5.3 Example of an Activity with both TF and FF
Activity B : The TF can be found by examing the network to be 4 days, ie the ES of activity F minus the duration of Activity B itself, $7 - 3 = 4$ days. The FF is given by $ES_{(succ)}$ – Earliest finishing time for $B = 7 - (0+3) = 4$ days. The reader could select activities not on the critical path and check as in the above examples to find the TF and FF associated with them.

6 PRESENTATION OF THE NETWORK IN THE FORM OF A GANTT CHART
A Gantt chart is a horizontal bar-chart superimposed upon a time scale.

This type of chart, in a variety of forms, has been used for many years as a planning tool. The advantages of transcribing the network into this form are:

(i) the time-scale can be translated into calendar time, or hours of the day, so assisting in the control of a project by observing the progress of activities against real time

(ii) it is a more readily understandable presentation to people unfamiliar with networks

(iii) a block frequency histogram can be built up at the foot of the chart and on the same time-scale to show the use of resources (labour, machinery, capital etc) and to show what advantages might be achieved by delaying or re-positioning non-critical activities

(iv) a clearer picture of the amounts of float available can be gained from this presentation.

7 USE OF THE GANTT CHART IN SCHEDULING AND ALLOCATING WORK

In relatively simple networks it is possible to move activities (taking care to preserve any logic sequences of activities) so that the resources are used at minimum cost, and to do this by inspection of the Gantt chart alone. For example, if it can be seen that at one point on the time-scale more labour is required than would be available, then the activities responsible for that labour requirement can be located on the chart above that point and non-critical activities moved along the time-scale so as to lessen labour requirements at that point. This is know at resource smoothing and can be a source of financial saving. Allocation of work to different members of staff is done once the resource levels have been smoothed and on the basis of the required grouping of skills.

8 EXAMPLE OF A NETWORK ANALYSIS APPLICATION

It has been decided to install a bar for beer and wine sales in a suitable hotel room currently in use as a residents' lounge.

The following activities are identified after tenders for the work have been received and the contract with the selected firm signed :

Preparation of bar floor area (2 days)
Plumbing – first fix (2 days)
Plumbing – second fix (2 days)
Electrics – first fix (1 day)
Plaster work (3 days)
Electrics – second fix (1 day)
Painting behind-bar walls and ceilings (2 days)
Completion of decor, mirror installation (3 days)
Erection of shelving (2 days)
Prefabrication of bar (off-site) (21 days)
Installation of bar (2 days)
Mounting and connection of beer pumps (1 day)

Order wines, spirits and beers (14 days)
Receive and stock wines, etc (1 day)
Laying of cork flooring (1 day)

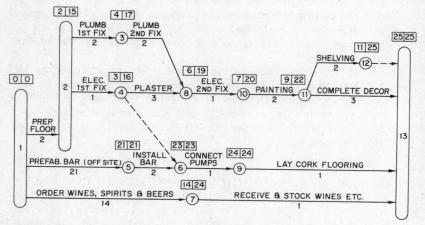

START NODE	END NODE	ACTIVITY	DAYS DURATION 1 2 3 4 5 6 7 8 9 10 11 12 13 14 15 16 17 18 19 20 21 22 23 24 25
1	2	PREP. FLOOR	
1	5	PREFAB. BAR	
1	7	ORDER STOCK	
2	3	PLUMB 1ST FIX	
2	4	ELEC. 1ST FIX	
3	8	PLUMB 2ND FIX	
4	8	PLASTER	
4	6	DUMMY	
5	6	INSTALL BAR	
6	9	CONN. PUMPS	
7	13	REC. STOCK	
8	10	ELEC. 2ND FIX	
9	13	FLOORING	
10	11	PAINTING	
11	12	SHELVING	
11	13	COMP. DECOR	
12	13	DUMMY	

8.1 Using the Gantt chart

The sequence of activities 1,5; 5,6; 6,9; 9,13 have durations which total to 25 days and, therefore, lie on the critical path. It can be seen that on the chart 1,5 starts at the beginning of day 1 (time zero) and the sequence continues to the end of day 25, the overall project time. Suppose that it is desired that the residents' lounge is to remain undisturbed for as long as possible before starting on the bar installation. Attention must be given to activities not on the critical path to calculate the length of time by which the non-critical activities could be delayed. If the preparation of the bar floor area is delayed for, say ten days, would the whole installation still be possible within the 25 days?

138

The sequences following the floor preparation are:
(i) 2,3; 3,8; 8,10; 10,11 and 11,13 (11,12 lies within the duration of 11,13). The total of these durations is 12 days, including the time for floor preparation, so the ten day delay + 12 = 22 days, which is within the overall project time.
(ii) 2,4; 4,8 also follow floor preparation, but their respective durations, 1 and 3 days, bring these two activities to the end of day 6 and into the sequence at (i), above at 8,10. Thus, all work in the room could be delayed for ten days and still have 3 days spare.

If the delay selected had been 13 days, it should be noted that all the activities would then have been critical, ie, lateness in any one of them would cause an over-run of the 25 day project time.

When several sequences are allowed to become critical it is easy to see that supervisory control over their progress becomes more difficult.

Up to this point day numbers only have been used, but if 'time zero' is given a date, then every activity could be dated as to its start and finish and the whole project could be dated as to its completion.

If this work is planned on the basis of a five-day week, then five weeks after its start is the target date when the bar should be open.

If, at this stage in the planning, it becomes clear that five weeks from the start date over-runs, say, a public holiday which offers good sales opportunity, then an examination of how the project time could be reduced can take place. The activities to examine are those on the critical path and of those, the pre-fabrication of the bar is the longest. The contractor could be approached to discuss the possibility of reducing the time by, for example, overtime working or minor modifications to design. This is likely to increase costs, so the decision as to whether to go for the higher cost, reduced time option would necessitate a forecast of the profit increase expected from an earlier opening date. If the expected profits outweigh the increased installation costs, then the contractor would be asked to proceed on the basis of the shortened schedule.

Any reduction in the duration of the critical path will need to be incorporated in the network to determine whether such reduction makes other activities critical.

Suppose that the contractor could reduce the pre-fabrication time by 10 days. The overall project time is now 15 days. Only one other sequence in this network has become critical and that is the calling in and stocking of the wines, spirits and beers. This time could be reduced simply by changing the source of supply – instead of an order to the supplier with a 14 day lead time, other sources of supply with almost immediate delivery could be used. Once again, this may increase costs, so that it is essential to weigh the extra cost of any decisions taken to ensure that the expected financial outcome of those decisions remains favourable. The Gantt chart shows that no other sequence is greater than 12 days duration so, although it is somewhat tighter than the original, 25 day project time, no problems are revealed.

139

The final point to notice on this Gantt chart is that freedom to move activities shown by the broken lines indicating total float.

In this case, any of the activities with float could be moved so that the end of the duration line is at the end of the float.

For example, if 3,8, Plumbing 2nd fix, is delayed until day 18, it will be completed by the end of day 19. This leaves 6 days to the end of the project and the sequence of Electrics 2nd fix, Paining and completion of Decor totals to the 6 days remaining.

Critical path activities are seen on the chart as the durations with no float attached to them.

8.2 The example of network analysis in section 8.1 above has been kept as simple as possible to enable the basic ideas of network analysis to be easily apparent. There are only 17 activities, including 2 dummy activities, in the network, so that it is possible to perform all the calculations of earliest starts and latest finishes, identify the critical path and draw and use the Gantt chart with no difficulty and in a short time.

If the project being networked has upwards of 80 activities, or if the dependencies of activities are complex and produce a complex critical path, then the task of determining that path, calculating floats, producing the Gantt chart and resource histograms and attempting to use the floats to smooth resource requirements may be too complex to carry out manually and a computer program may be necessary.

There are many such programs available, some of which can be used on a micro-computer of 32K capacity.

In using the program with which the authors are most familiar, the stages in preparing the computer input are given below.

9 USING COMPUTER ASSISTANCE IN NETWORK ANALYSIS

Before preparing the computer input, the network must be completed and the activity durations checked for reliability.

The input can now be assembled under the following headings:

| Activity Number | Start Node | End Node | Duration | Resources | | Activity Name |
				Labour	Machine	

The program is in conversational mode, so that having loaded and entered the total number of activities (including dummies) the questions appear on the visual display unit in the order of the above headings as to start and end numbers, durations, etc, and answers are keyed in appropriately.

On completion of the input the critical path, project duration and float values are computed and the print-out gives the following information:

duration of project
the critical path node numbers
earliest starts and latest finishes for all activities
total float on each activity.

At the foot of the first print out is a Gantt chart on a suitably selected time-scale, graphically depicting the durations by double lines and the existence of float by single lines.

Below the Gantt chart a resource histogram is drawn showing, for example the required numbers of staff along the same time-scale as the Gantt chart and calculated on the basis provided by the network.

This program has been frequently used by students who have networked the kitchen activities necessary to the support of their kitchen projects menus. At the end of the first print-out it is common to find a calculated requirement for a large number of kitchen staff.

This is because many menus embody a large number of activities which could be started together because they are not dependent on anything going before. Once the print-out is available, the user then writes in against selected activities the amount of time by which each should be delayed. The guides to which activities can be delayed are the calculated float values and the selection of the activities for:

(i) technological reasons (eg dishes which should be made as late as possible so as to be served fresh and at the right temperature)

(ii) work allocation purposes, when the main reason for placing an activity at a given time on the scale is to create an even workload

(iii) making the best use of available equipment.

The next stage of the program is the input of the new information as to the activities to be delayed and the amount of each delay. If the initial information put into the computer is correct, then the logic sequences following any delayed activity will be preserved.

The next print-out from the computer includes the delays and shows a new Gantt chart with activities repositioned as required and a new resource histogram showing the effect of the delays upon staff and equipment requirements throughout the length of the project.

If the delays have been thoughtfully selected it is often possible in this application to make final adjustments on the Gantt chart manually, producing a reasonable and workable control plan for the project and using a minimum number of staff.

At first sight it might seem that a one-off menu production is not particularly suitable for an application of network analysis.

Yet if a cyclic menu in, perhaps, an institutional situation is considered, then a set of networks based on reliable standard times could be a valuable aid to control in the kitchen. Any new dishes introduced into menus could quickly be tested as to the effect upon workloads or equipment resources. If the changes are indicated as calling for staff increases then the kitchen management have sufficient time to revise the recipes to decrease, if possible, work content. If it is not possible, then there can be second thoughts on the inclusion of the new dish.

Similarly, network for banquets and functions provide check-lists and schedules of activities which can be valuable in ensuring the smooth running of these services.

10 SUGGESTED APPLICATIONS OF NETWORK ANALYSIS

Basically, any complex of activities which employs people whose activities are interdependent is a candidate for network analysis. In the hotel and catering industry the following applications have possibilities:

(i) clerical procedures such as the drafting and progressing of budgets or the closure of books of account and preparation of final accounts

(ii) the periodic closure of parts of an hotel for thorough cleaning or refurbishment to keep disturbance to a minimum

(iii) planning the installation of work study findings when the purchase of new equipment, operator and supervisory training and new wages systems are involved

(iv) kitchen organisation and control as described in section 9

(v) the type of project control described in section 8

(vi) planning an advertising and sales promotion campaign to ensure date tie-up between the campaign and the availability of the advertised facilities.

It is hoped that enough information on network analysis has been given to indicate its value as part of a manager's tool-kit.

The calculation of float values and the analysis of float into its different classifications has been touched upon only, partly for reasons of space and partly because computer assistance makes float calculation rather more of an academic question than when the technique user tackled the job manually.

A further short-cut has been the acceptance of single time durations for each activity. A moment's thought is enough to realise that time estimates could be subject to variation. For each activity there could be a time under the most favourable conditions, a most likely time and a time under the least favourable conditions. Simulation techniques and other methods employing mathematical probability can be used to deal with these variations but their description and methods of application absorbe more space than is available for this introduction to network analysis. Nevertheless, it is believed that this chapter gives enough basic information to enable anyone interested to experiment with the technique and thereby appreciate more fully the benefits it offers in the planning, controlling and co-ordinating of the activities in a project.

Further reading:

WOODGATE, H S, *Planning by Network,* 3rd edn, 1977, Business Books Ltd.

12
Conclusion

A difficulty associated with any text-book is that for the purpose of explanation, the whole is divided into parts which are studied as separate units or activities, and that in this process the perspective of the whole may be lost.

This brief note attempts to pull together the various aspects of 'management' examined in the text.

Any business must operate within its internal and external environments and is influenced and constrained by legislation, resources and many other factors. It is in the light of these environments that a company determines the objectives it will pursue at corporate, departmental, sectional and individual levels.

To determine objectives, decisions must be made as to their nature. This decision making process requires that an adequate data base be provided for the decision makers and requires information as to the total situation within the company, about the market and all other aspects of the environment in which it is to operate and of any changes taking place within it.

Objectives having been formulated, policies and plans can be developed by means of which the objectives can be attained. Policies, rules and regulations determine the way in which the company will order its internal affairs and set down how the various activities will be conducted, stipulating what must be done, or not done, and where discretion may be exercised. Plans are the means by which objectives should be realised, and sections within the company will each have their own plans to realise their own, specific objectives. These specific plans and objectives are complementary to each other and in total combine to achieve the overall objectives of the organisation within the time-scale laid down.

Planning involves people and what people are to do. In determining the plans for departments, sections and people, the function of delegation involves allocating specific tasks to individuals. This may be as straightforward as it sounds or may involve the technique of Management by Objectives, where individuals take part in the setting of their own objectives.

The two activities of planning and delegation, deciding how objectives are to be tackled and by whom, effectively determines the structure of the organisation itself. Decisions as to the nature and number of sections and departments required to achieve objectives is part of the planning process and this, coupled with the determination of individual responsibilities creates the framework of the organisation.

Planning and delegation, however, fragment the work and involve specialisation of both departments and individuals. It therefore becomes necessary that this sub-divided work, done by specialists, is re-unified or co-ordinated at the appropriate times and places. Some writers consider that co-ordination is not just one of the functions of management, but is the total management activity and that by definition one who co-ordinates is a manager. Whatever views are taken of this, what is not arguable is that co-ordination cannot be achieved without communication.

Communication, in whatever form, is the means by which all the separate activities can be properly combined. The principal means of effecting co-ordination is, of course, the manager.

All the operations of the organisation require a control process to ensure that all does go according to plan, that deviations are detected and either performance or plans modified. As a result of control, and of comparing performance with plans, information is generated providing the data base against which both performance and objectives can be evaluated and, if necessary modified in preparation for the next cycle of activities.

Additionally, Purchasing and Materials Management and Work Study have been dealt with as specific managerial tools used within the overall managerial framework.

Within the constraints of a short book, it has not been possible to cover any specific aspect of management in any depth. However, sufficient has been said about all aspects of management to enable the student to appreciate the totality of the management function in the hotel and catering industry.

Index